# THE

# PARENTING

# TIGHT-

# ROPE

# THE PARENTING TIGHT-ROPE

## A Flexible Approach To Building Self-Esteem

**By Julie Stitt**

**Foreword by James Windell**

Momentum Books Ltd.

Manufactured in the United States of America

1997  1996  1995  1994      5  4  3  2  1

Momentum Books, Ltd.
6964 Crooks Road, Suite 1
Troy, Michigan  48098
USA

ISBN 1-879094-31-2

Library of Congress Cataloging-in-Publication Data

Stitt, Julie, 1947-
    The parenting tightrope : a flexible approach to building
self-esteem / by Julie Stitt.
            p.    cm.
    Includes biographical references (p.              ).
    ISBN 1-879094-31-2 : $9.95
    1. Child rearing.  2. Self-esteem in children.  3. Parent and
teenager.  4. Parent and child.  I. Title.
HQ772.S76   1994
649'.1--dc20                                              94-33909

# ~*Dedication*~

To my own family and other families facing parenting challenges everywhere.

*~ The Parenting Tightrope ~*

# ~ *Table of Contents* ~

# ~ *Table of Contents* ~

# ~Foreword~

All parents come to the task of raising children with love and a desire to bring up a healthy, happy child. And I've found in working with adolescents over the years that young people frequently set goals related to the kind of parent they'd like to be, often planning to bring their own children up differently from the way they were raised.

Perhaps most of us approach the job of parenting in just this way. We set out to be better parents than our own parents and hope to be both nurturing and wise with our children. What we learn all too quickly, once on the job, is that it isn't quite that easy. As always, having more knowledge of the pitfalls and the stresses of a situation gives us a healthier respect for those who have done the job previously.

When that job is parenting, we learn what a delicate balancing act this business of raising children is. As Julie Stitt, the author if this wonderfully gentle and lucid book points out, parenting is like walking a tightrope and trying to keep one's balance despite the forces that tend to contribute to unbalance.

With her recognition that most parents approach the task of parenting with care, love, and a desire to do well, the author has set out to guide parents in channeling all of that positive energy in appropriate ways. I'm happy to be able to say that she accomplishes this task exceptionally well. She's presented the major aspects of parenting in a simple, direst, and tolerant way. In her writing she displays a remarkable warm style that has undoubtedly made her a successful parent of her own children while offering the parents who are looking for a new book a particularly valuable guide to raising children.

While she makes the well-travelled parenting ground of communication, expectations, discipline and values sound fresh, she also covers some territory that is not so well trod. These latter areas include helping children appreciate the differences among people and coping with parent-child conflict.

The author has considerable experience in working with children in crisis and a whole section of her book deals with common crises experienced by children and families. This is a useful addition to the parenting advice that's so readily available these days.

I believe this book will be a valuable reference for many parents in raising healthy and peaceful children from toddlerhood to adolescence. I'm proud to welcome Julie Stitt to the ranks of acknowledged parenting experts who are writing for that vast number of mothers and fathers who want to be competent, skilled, and successful parents but who need help on occasion with the inevitable questions or concerns that unsettles most of us parents.

—James Windell, author
*Eight Weeks to a Well-Behaved Child*

# ~ *Acknowledgments* ~

I would like to take this opportunity to thank the many people who helped make this book possible. Writing a book on parenting became a realistic goal after my colleague Marcy Haney introduced me to her husband Bill Haney of Momentum Books. Kyle Scott then facilitated the coordination of production at Momentum. Special thanks are due to Tom Ferguson, who edited the first draft of the manuscript and provided detailed critiques to guide my revisions.

I would also like to thank my husband Ebony Stitt and my father Dr. Harold Goodman, who gave generously of their time and provided many suggestions for clarifying ideas; Juanita B. Bowman, MA, MSW, ACSW at Children's Hospital of Michigan provided valuable additions for the chapter on "Children with Special Needs" and Dr. Alice McCarthy, president of the Center for the Advancement of the Family, provided materials for the bibliography and encouraged me to keep writing.

Much of the subject matter for this book is taken directly from the *Watch Me Grow* and *Project Self* program manuals I authored previously. Drs. Jordan and Margaret Paul and Virginia Satir are just a few of the authors from whom permission was obtained for utilizing their perspectives on human interaction. I would also like to thank the facilitators of these programs and the participating families, who provided a wealth of experiences for me to consider in creating this book.

Additionally, I would like to thank Common Ground Director Tony Rothschild, the board and the staff for their support in making this book a reality.

Last, but certainly not least, I would like to thank my family — my immediate family for putting up with me when the pressure was on and continuing their love and support and my extended family for all their sharing and caring over the years that helped me understand the importance of family enough to write this book.

# ~ *Introduction* ~

If there is a tougher job than raising a child, I don't know what it might be.

In fact, one of life's amazements is that a job driven by love and caring rather than by a paycheck can be so difficult.

And so important.

Parenting can be lonely at times, even in a crowded home. And, as you strive so hard to do the right thing, it can be confusing. *Very* confusing.

On the one hand, some "experts" tell you that children are having such a hard time in today's scary world because parents have been too permissive. It's because kids are spoiled, these experts say — that they lack the discipline to "just" say no.

At the same time, other "experts" tell you that an authoritarian, my-way-or-the-highway approach encourages rebellion. Your kids must learn to think for themselves to make healthy decisions, these experts say.

Where does that leave a frustrated parent? Walking a "precarious parenting" tightrope between those two poles — often uncertain even of which direction to aim each tentative, wary step.

Sometimes it is tempting to avoid this balancing act by saying: "Well, maybe we parents don't make that much difference anyway." Can we really influence how our kids turn out? Or is that quirk in your son or daughter's temperament something inherited from a relative about whom you only heard stories. Or are youth strictly a product of their peer group?

In my view, a parent who works hard at this most difficult of jobs can make a world of difference. Yes, every situation is different. Yes, every child is different. Yes, life in the ghetto is very different from life in an affluent suburb. Yes, you might "do the right thing" and still wind up with serious problems on your hands. But parents remain the real VIPs in youngsters' lives.

Accepting that life has given you this tightrope to walk, this balancing act to carry off, is the key to effective parenting. Flexibility is your strongest tool.

No single course of action is going to work in every situation. You must master a variety of techniques, and then keep them handy. Otherwise, you'll be like a chef who uses the same three spices in every recipe.

Already you know where the title of this book came from. And you know that I am going to suggest some paths to flexibility as you struggle with your own balancing act.

Your next question probably should be: "Who is this author to be telling me how to raise my child?" It's a fair question that requires a two-part answer.

First, I'm not trying to "tell you how to raise your son or daughter." Certainly not in a strictly prescriptive, step-by-step way. If I did, I wouldn't be setting a very good example of flexibility. Instead, I hope to offer you some effective ways of channeling that vast reservoir of love and care that you, as a parent, already possess. I'll share with you some examples, from all the different stages of "growing up," but I don't pretend for a minute that your own situation — whatever it may be — doesn't have its own special twist.

Second, I have worked with youth in both recreational and educational settings for 2 1/2 decades. I have worked with youngsters who were ready to drop out of school and those who were "gifted" and achieving well. Some of my students have spoken English as a second language; some were classified as learning disabled. I've worked in the inner city; I've worked in suburbia.

Currently, I am prevention services director at Common Ground, a 24-hour crisis intervention agency in Royal Oak, Michigan, a Detroit suburb. During my nine years at Common Ground, time and again it has been made clear to me that parents in all communities need more tools and support for this daunting task of raising healthy children. And that is true whether a youngster is aged three, 10 or 16.

Among the youths who call the Common Ground crisis lines for help — dealing with issues ranging from conflict with their parents, to drugs or alcohol, to suicidal thoughts, to an urge to run away from home — a common thread is prevalent: low self-esteem. How can kids hope to make their way through life's many hurdles if they don't feel good about who they are?

Some people view this "belief in oneself," as it's defined by Webster, in a narrow sense, as if it were confined to the individual. But I think parents must recognize the influence the whole community has on our kids' self-esteem. How children are treated not only by parents, but by teachers, their peers and others they care about are merged in the picture they paint of themselves. I believe that low self-esteem is at the root of many child and adolescent difficulties, of a serious nature or not.

Our children need to like themselves if we want them to get along well with others and work through problem situations. It's a simple idea, but seldom is it easily achieved. Otherwise, good kids from all kinds of homes wouldn't be on our crisis lines needing help.

Common Ground has responded with three programs — *Project Self, Watch Me Grow* and *Peer Relationships* — that are being used in schools, successfully, to raise self-esteem by building life skills. What we're doing in the schools, however, needs reinforcement from those Very Important People: you, the parents. It is because parents must become more involved in consciously sharing life skills with their children that we decided to offer this book as a resource.

Please believe me when I say that I understand the challenges faced by both parents and children in a world that is changing in almost incomprehensible ways, at almost incomprehensible speed. I am writing this book not only as a professional, but as a parent. I'm the working mother of two daughters (ages seven and twelve) and a seventeen-year-old stepson, who lives with me. Four other stepchildren are grown. For three years now, I have been a grandmother.

Parenting mistakes? No one has as many opportunities as parents to make mistakes. So all of us make them. That includes parents working double shifts to make ends meet, and affluent parents for whom time is not a luxury. It includes people who have never given much though to parenting, and professionals — like myself — who have devoted their lives to the subject.

At some point, all of us yell at our children, or punish them inappropriately. At some other point, we all let them "slide" when we shouldn't. Lucky for us, these mistakes can be offset later in a number of ways that soften the impact. Parenting, it turns out, involves much on-the-job learning. On average, the job will last eighteen years — assuming you have only one child.

Leading our children to see themselves as valuable, contributing members of our diverse society is a goal I plan to strive toward for my entire life. A very large number of professionals, paraprofessionals and volunteers share that goal, and also are devoting their best efforts to the task.

Absolutely the most significant difference any professional

can make, however, is to bring the parents firmly and constructively into the picture. Most parents want to be there, but they need information and support. You would not be reading these words if you hadn't already enlisted in the cause.

So with an eye to the joys and rewards that accompany and outweigh the sorrows and frustrations of parenting, the following chapters are intended to make your on-the-job training go a little more smoothly.

I said these pages would not be prescriptive, but they will not be of much use if we talk of nothing but generalities. So each chapter will highlight a specific component of building healthy self-esteem. I'll be drawing liberally from situations every parent encounters, situations where you're not sure what to do, what will work, what effect it will have on your youngster down the road. I'll explore some methods of dealing with these situations, and I'll try to explain why they're reasonable choices.

In some sections I'll be dealing with specific age groups, but the dynamics tend to be useful for all parents to think about.

Remember, no matter what, nothing is so important as having our children know that we love them and are concerned about their well-being.

I think you already know that. But isn't it amazing how difficult it can be to communicate that most important and positive of all facts of life?

This book is designed to help.

*~ The Parenting Tightrope ~*

# ~ *Part One* ~

# Basics for Building Self-Esteem

Children may enter the world with Dad's nose, Mom's dimple and a whole lot of temperament that seems built-in, but as parents we have a great deal of influence over how our children develop a concept of themselves — their self-esteem, an intricate image of mental, physical and social characteristics.

Helping children formulate a healthy picture of themselves is not a simple process. Our own ability as parents to nurture our children inevitably has been influenced by how we were treated as youngsters. If one grew up in a situation in which acceptance and love were freely given, nurturing children might come almost naturally. If one lived in an environment in which feelings often were denied and being judged was the norm, it may be difficult not to continue the same behavior. Of course, most of us grew up in situations that included both approaches.

Regardless, without positive feedback, it is difficult for youngsters to learn to value themselves. If children get the impression from you that parenting is primarily a chore and a responsibility, they will tend to see themselves in a negative light — as a burden. If they don't value themselves, it's unlikely they'll

1

value — or respect — others. In conveying a positive attitude to children, flexibility is a valuable tool. No one response, type of discipline or method of molding behavior is going to work all the time. Techniques that work at one point with a particular child may not work later. Being equipped with a wide variety of tools can help.

Sometimes it's difficult for parents to fully recognize the strong connection between the life skills that are the foundation of healthy self-esteem and a child's resistance to negative behavior. But, think about it. Who do you think would be more susceptible to drug abuse or delinquency — a confident, self-assured youngster who felt valued, respected and loved by friends and family and had been trained in healthy decision making or a youngster who was struggling for acceptance and love and had always been told by others what to do? Each child deserves parents who are willing to put effort into helping him or her learn to contribute to society in a healthy way.

The first section of this book contains basic skills — helpful approaches for building a structure with clear expectations and consistent boundaries. Parents need to keep in mind as they read that having a positive outlook and being willing to share and have fun are also important for healthy parenting.

## ~ *Chapter One* ~

# Communicating

**I**magine you have been taken prisoner on another planet. You don't understand the language spoken, and all the natives are at least three times your size. Even knowing everything you know as an adult, how would you handle such a situation? Would you be frightened by the size of these beings and your inability to control them? Would you feel frustrated trying to communicate? Would you be comfortable depending on your captives for food and water? Would you resent them limiting your movements?

Infants do not see their parents as foreign beings. As children grow, however, they feel many of the same emotions as that captive on another planet. How many times, for instance, have you seen a small child being dragged through a store, one arm stretched up in the air, being screamed at by someone three times his or her size, who was refusing to listen to what the youngster was trying to say? And this is the same person on whom the child is dependent for food, clothing, shelter and love.

Parents who want to promote healthy communication should think about how their statements and actions might look from a child's point of view. This adds perspective in evaluating the messages sent, exploring ways open up two-way communication and thinking specifically about how to encourage children to participate actively in the communications process.

## Three Ways to Send a Message

The words we choose are the most obvious kind of communication. But what gets received at the other end is affected not only by *what* we say, but *how fast* we say it, *how loud* and our *tone* of voice. *Content*, or the specific words, is not always what makes the difference. In fact, it's more often *how* the words were said.

For example, "I see you made your bed" can be a pleasant compliment. These same words also can be a sarcastic put-down. What a drastic difference using "identical" words! Working as a counselor, I have met parents who even in casual conversations were clearly passing judgment on me. It all came through in the tone of their voice. Can you imagine the pressure on their children? It must be hard to feel that people on whom you depend for love constantly view you with a critical eye. This kind of interaction makes it difficult for children to believe in themselves.

It is, of course, a two-way street. Teens who imply with their tone of voice that everything their parents try to include them in is "boring" have a strong influence on communication also, none of it good.

The faces we make, eye contact, how we move, and the distance we keep all are forms of *nonverbal communication.*

These signals are every bit as important to our messages as the words we use.

How many parents remember their children's faces when they first learned to play hide and seek? I truly knew how powerful *nonverbal communication* could be when I looked at my first daughter just after her birth. I was still on the delivery table after Amanda had been washed up, wrapped in a blanket and had a little cap put on her head. The nurse laid her by my side. When I looked down at her, she just stared directly back at me for the longest time. It was a precious moment. And I have no doubt that our communication began at that instant.

Nonverbal messages can be immensely effective. My mother sometimes used a look we called "Number 37." When she got this look, we knew we'd better shape up right away or we'd be in serious trouble. Just mentioning the number, however, letting her know that we had gotten her message, seemed to break the tension. It's by no means easy, but everyone must try to be aware of the nonverbal messages being communicated in their families.

Sighs, grunts, groans and laughter also send information or change what we feel about a verbal message. This third way of getting messages across is called *paralingual communication*: sounds we make that aren't words. For instance, a teen might say to a parent, "It's OK. I'll babysit tonight, even though there's a game," but then sigh heavily. The words say it's OK, but the sigh says something else.

Being conscious of all three types of communication — our choice of words and nonverbal and paralingual communication — is a good starting point in the never-ending challenge of exchanging real messages with our children. But before polishing those skills, you'll find it useful to recognize some common types of behavior that can prevent healthy communication. And you *will* recognize them.

## Roadblocks to Communication

I don't know how many parents have told me: "My kids used to talk to me all the time, but they stopped once they became teenagers." As teenagers, the parents will assert, kids talk only when they want something.

On the other hand, teens tell me they don't talk to their parents because they don't like always being told what to do or that they have done something wrong.

Listen closely the next time you're in a store. You'll frequently find parents setting up roadblocks something like this: "Johnny, get back over here. Don't touch that. I told you to keep an eye on your brother. Now, see what he's done. If you'd done what I told you to, this never would have happened. You're no help at all. I just wish you'd mind." This constant negative attitude is bad enough in the added stress of public situations. Unfortunately, I've often heard the same kind of talk in the "comfort" of homes.

It's important to remember that "real" communication is an *exchange* of information. For communication to happen at all, both parties must be *willing* to make the exchange. At times, however, what comes more naturally to many of us are phrases that actually set up *roadblocks to two-way communication.*

Virginia Satir, a nationally known family therapist, thoroughly explores family interaction in her book, *Peoplemaking.* She has categorized four specific roles as setting up some of the most common barriers to communication. Both children and adults sometimes fall into these roles. Know the enemy: become familiar with these types behavior in order to avoid them.

The example of the parent in the story typifies the role of a *Blamer*: someone who sees himself or herself as perfect and blames someone else when anything goes wrong. They're great at shaking that finger no matter where they are.

Satir characterizes the Blamer as a dictator, a boss, who acts superior and seems to be saying, "If it weren't for you everything would be all right." The Blamer's face is tense and the voice hard, tight and, often, shrill.

It's so easy for parents to blame their kids for every sort of problem, big or trivial. After all, they're smaller than we are, so they can't fight back very well. Most parents don't like themselves when they fall into this role; but, like many bad habits, it's so easy to do. Keep your eyes open and you'll see it everywhere, like violence in cartoons. The Blamer attitude can be devastating to children who must endure it very often.

Sometimes youngsters fall into Blamer patterns, too. Occasionally, they'll try to send adults on a guilt trip. More often, they'll blame their peers for something that's gone wrong. Siblings also famous for using this technique on each other: "I didn't do anything! It's all Sammy's fault! He's always picking on me."

Satir labels her second characterization the *Computer.* These people are always right, just like the Blamer. But the Computer feels so superior that he or she won't stoop to showing emotion. Computer types can judge you silently with a special searing look that says: "I am very reasonable, cool, calm and collected." The Computer's long, perfectly correct sentences are rattled off in a monotone.

For example, a Computer parent looking at a child's poor report card might say something like: "It greatly displeases me to see these horrendous grades. It is obvious that you have not been properly utilizing the intellectual abilities with which you were fortunate enough to have been graced. It dismays me to think of the implications to your future that a continuance of this type of behavior might involve." It's difficult to capture Computer talk, but you get the picture.

7

The third type is the *Placater,* for whom almost anything goes. A Placater might say: "It's OK if you don't do your homework now, if you promise you'll get it done later. Just don't tell your Dad when he gets home. I don't want any trouble. And don't tell him about that note your teacher sent home. I'll take care of that tomorrow. Just be good, so we can have a nice evening."

The Placater always talks to please, often apologizes, almost never disagrees. This is a certified "yes" person. Their voices lean toward a whine or squeak as "yes" is said in an effort to avoid trouble. Kids with Placater parents can get away with anything — including changing their minds and manipulation — because their parents are so concerned about keeping the "peace." Kids who are Placaters are sometimes seen as "goody two-shoes," always trying to please and to "behave" without resistance.

The last type Satir describes is the *Distracter.* The Distracter is so busy doing other things, there's no time to stop and really pay attention to what others are saying. The Distracter always misses the point and says or does things irrelevant to what anyone else is saying or doing. After all, there are bills to pay, dinners to fix and TV Guides to be studied. Not answering questions directly and changing the subject are the Distracter's specialty. The Distracter's voice tends to be out of focus, singsonging up and down without reason.

For example, a child might try to tell a Distracter parent about what he or she did at school and get this response: "Oh, you drew a picture in art today? I've been meaning to get someone to come in to redecorate the living room. I'm tired of the way it looks. Would you like a snack? I've got to start supper. What did you say you did in math today?" Kids can be champion

Distracters, too, particularly when they're watching TV or playing a video game.

Satir's four personality types describe, to one degree or another, people we all know. Now, here are four additional types of *behavior* that we all recognize, which also prevent two-way communication. Parents sometimes use these roadblocks deliberately, sometimes inadvertently. Either way, the results tend to be the same.

*Generalizing:* By saying things such as, "You're *always* breaking things!" or "You *never* keep your room clean!" parents can make children feel hopeless, facing overwhelming odds. Name-calling goes hand-in-hand with generalizing.

*Expressing negative expectations:* Such statements as, "You can try, but you're just too little," or "You'll never be able to do that" set kids up for failure. Just remember: Your kids are likely to meet your expectations.

*Criticizing judgmentally or accusing:* "You should have ..." or "How could you have ...?" are common phrases used in this judgmental mode. Parents frequently assume things to be true before checking out the facts. Then when the wrong headed parent moves on to share his or her life experiences, the words of wisdom fall on deaf ears.

*Warning or threatening:* "If you don't, then I'll ..." and "You had better ... or else" are probably heard in every grocery store at least a dozen times a day. This is a favorite method of many parents, who apparently don't remember *The Boy Who Cried Wolf*.

Still other roadblocks to two-way communication include *lecturing and interrogating*. Both techniques give the impression that a parent feels superior and is in the power seat. With older kids particularly, this is like issuing a handwritten invitation to test the limits.

The roles characterized by Virginia Satir and the techniques just described create stress for all concerned. Two-way communication becomes impossible. The person on the receiving end believes his or her replies won't be heard, even if he or she tries to answer. And that's probably right.

## Effective Communication

Feeling tongue-tied? Once a roadblock approach becomes a habit, telling someone to avoid these barriers can be like telling them not to talk. So, is two-way communication really possible between parents and children? After twenty-five years of working with children and their parents as a educator, I strongly believe the answer to that question is "YES!"

Before we get into the specifics of two-way communication, however, I'd like to emphasize the necessity of *exchange* for there to be "real" communication. Nothing illustrates this as well as a story I heard at a workshop years ago. A child with normal hearing was born to two deaf parents. Social workers worried about the baby learning to talk, since both parents spoke only through sign language. So, the child was scheduled to watch — and listen to — television every day. However, the toddler still did not learn to speak. His ability to sign, on the other hand, developed early and effectively. He hadn't learned voice communication because learning to communicate requires exchange, an acknowledgment from others of common terms to express ourselves. Appropriate opportunities were then offered to this child.

Keep this in mind as we think about how to really communicate with our children. Virginia Satir describes two-way communication as "leveling." When you level with someone, communication is honest. Verbal and nonverbal messages flow in the same direction. Mixed messages that express one thing verbally, but something else nonverbally or paralingually, have no place in leveling. Both parties are willing to talk and listen *actively.* Conversations in which there is leveling:

- Are real and straightforward, describing specifically and directly what is meant.
- Represent the truth at that moment.
- Express a whole feeling, not a partial one — for instance, the worry that often precedes anger is expressed along with the anger.

Children tend to be sensitive to whether or not people are honest with them. All of us sometimes have mixed feelings and will legitimately send mixed messages because our emotions are confused. But sending mixed messages without explanation often confuses others and undermines their sense of trust, as well as eroding confidence in their own ability to understand what is happening around them. Being conscious of this dynamic is important.

For example, a mother who watches her child going to take a first swimming lesson might say: "Oh, it's so much fun to learn to swim. You're really going to like it." However, a child may sense nervousness in her mother's body language, if Mom's actually somewhat afraid of water herself. An explanation is important.

When analyzing the communications process, it's important to distinguish between the objective and subjective levels. The word content represents the objective realm of communication. The subjective part of the message requires interpretation by the receiver. It is relayed mainly through nonverbal and paralingual means.

Four very useful tools in keeping two-way communication going are *attending, perceiving, interpreting* and *getting feedback*. Here is a rundown on each.

## Attending

Healthy two-way communication requires making connections with those around us. Paying attention to what the other person is saying is often indicated through body movement. We show interest easily by facing our children or others directly and making eye contact when we talk to them. Touch, such as taking someone's hand, can also be used to show feelings of openness and a willingness to listen. A quiet place is ideal for conversation, but not always necessary or possible. If a child brings up a serious issue in a crowded room or during a rushed time, interest and respect can be shown by suggesting another place or time to talk.

## Perceiving

When my sister was nine, she came home from a girlfriend's house one day smelling like cigarette smoke. My mother immediately launched an "investigation" and discovered that my sister indeed had been experimenting with tobacco in her friend's basement. She was caught by a nose. It's useful for parents to remember that *perceiving* involves collecting information through *all* our senses.

Clues to better understanding can be picked up by carefully observing how people move. A pat on the arm or touch can show empathy. Smell, as with the smoking scenario, can tell us what someone has been doing. Taste has allowed parents to know with a kiss that their children were sick. Even the "sixth sense" of intuition shouldn't be ignored. For example, how often do parents correctly "sense" that their child is trying to hide something? Such clues are all part of the communications process.

## Interpreting

All parents have been in situations where they thought they knew exactly what their child was saying, only to find out later that they could not be farther off base. *Interpreting* the information we gather is especially a challenge when parents and children try to communicate. Previous experiences can't help but color the messages they send and receive. Attempts are made to hide feelings. Everyone says what they think the other wants to hear, instead of what they mean. Embarrassment, guilt and fear of admitting anger are just a few of the emotions lurking beneath statements, making interpretation difficult.

Unspoken messages can trigger unconscious reactions.

For example, a parent has a particularly frustrating day at the office. That evening, a child senses the negative feelings and lack of patience and becomes cranky. Worse yet, the child easily could interpret the feelings as his or her fault — when the real source lies miles and hours away!

Parents sometimes believe they know their youngsters so well that Mom and Dad can interpret messages without much thought. However, we need to be aware of the potential for communication foulups, especially as our children increase contact with others outside our homes.

A few years ago, the mother of a teen who participated in one of our small group programs called to say that she and her daughter had endured a terrible fight the previous evening as Mom drove daughter home from the group.

She asked her daughter what had been done in the group session. The daughter rattled off a long list of activities, all focused on listening skills. Then she challenged her mother to repeat it all — a test to see if she had really listened. According to the mother, she proceeded to recount what the daughter had said remarkably well. Then Mom asked, "How'd I do?" The daughter replied, "OK."

The mother got furious. "What do you mean, I only did "OK"? I repeated almost every word you said."

What the mother didn't understand at first, but agreed as we talked, was that her interpretation of "OK" was not the same as her daughter's. I often tell parents that if a teen says you've done *anything* "OK", you've done a great job. Getting a compliment from a teen can be like winning the million-dollar lotto. In this case, "OK" was another example of how taking just a minute to think about what a teen's or child's perspective might be can head off painful miscommunication.

The gender of parents and children also can affect communication and message interpretation. If this seems hard to swallow, do your own survey. Ask five men and five women what is meant by "I'm sorry." I'll bet you'll find a difference. In Deborah Tanner's book *You Just Don't Understand,* gender differences in interaction are documented. Examples range from topics such as occupational expectations projected by parents for their babies to dominance in adult business meetings. The need to make connections and indicate similarities is suggested as the dominant force for females. For males, sharing information and competing tend to be primary in conversations.

My eleven- and sixteen-year-old children illustrated these gender differences when I asked them to listen to a presentation I was planning for a school group. As I spoke, my daughter focused her eyes on me directly, interrupted to ask questions and nodded her head in agreement. My son doodled and didn't seem to pay attention. However, when I got to the part of the presentation when I asked them questions, my son had just as many answers as my daughter. Both gave me excellent suggestions about how to change the presentation to make it better. But was this a gender difference at work?

Quite possibly. My husband frequently used to tell our son to look at him as the two of them talked. I think that was uncomfortable for our son and actually shut him up. In our society, males tend to deal with each other in physically less direct ways than females do — but that doesn't mean they're not communicating, as my son's helpful comments proved.

Think about how men and women interact in public. It's much more common and acceptable for women to hug or touch. At a holiday celebration I attended recently, two men supported their common goals by hugging at the end of the presentation. Then one man took the time to reaffirm that they both were "real" men. I have never seen two females compelled to comment on such a physical display of affection. Boys and girls observe these differences, and respond in kind. Parents can promote health by analyzing interaction in our society, being accepting of differences that aren't harmful, and encouraging children to learn the best of both male and female communication techniques.

## Feedback

Regardless of their gender, asking children for *feedback* is a great tool for seeing if what was *heard* was really what was *meant*.

Two good ways for parents to get feedback are:

- Ask questions to get more information or make something clear.
- Paraphrase, putting what you heard in your own words.

"Tentifiers" can make obtaining feedback easier. Tentifiers are short phrases that give others the opportunity to say whether your perceptions were accurate or not, without being disagreeable. For example, a parent might say, "I hear you saying that you really don't like your art teacher." The child might respond with either, "No, it's just that the other kids in that class tease me," or, "Yes, and I don't think she likes me at all."

Using words that imply you are seeking information encourages children to share what they're feeling. Even if your perception was wrong, there's no feeling of being disagreed with personally. Other examples of tentifiers include, "It seems like ...," "Am I understanding that ...," and "It sounds as if ..." These phrases may seem a little contrived at first, but they really do open the door to two-way communication.

## Respecting Feelings

Think about your interaction with other adults. What kinds of situations make you feel angry, hurt or unhappy? Some of the most difficult situations are those in which our feelings are not respected by another person. Getting feedback under those circumstances is nearly impossible.

Yet, how many times have we heard a parent say to a child who has fallen: "Oh, stop crying. It doesn't hurt that much. You'll be all right!"

Our society encourages us to deny, rather than acknowledge, physical pain. Denying emotional pain is even more widespread. Many people do so to protect themselves from discomfort or from fear and hurt. Two-way conversations usually end, however, when the feelings of others are denied or someone tells another person how to think or feel.

Open communication, on the other hand, can be encouraged if parents acknowledge the feelings expressed first. "It sure is a pain when someone grabs a toy. Want some help figuring another way for both of you to get a turn?" Improvements for the situation can then be discussed.

With a physical injury, assistance might be as simple as applying a bandage. For emotional pain, first aid might mean developing a plan for making-up after a fight with a best friend. While helping a child explore ways to improve things, suggestions made impersonally often are more acceptable. Ideas presented this way keep children from feeling they have to contradict a parent directly, if they don't want to follow the suggestion, in the same way tentifiers do. For instance, a parent might say: "When some people get into this situation, they try ..." This structure also encourages children to begin learning to brainstorm solutions.

Tentifiers often keep the door open for sharing feelings without a specific solution in mind. "You seem kind of sad. Is there something wrong?"

## Trust

Acknowledging feelings effectively and showing respect consistently allows children to develop a trusting relationship with their parents. Two-way communication can then grow.

Some adults don't believe children need to be respected — that they can just be told what to do without explanation, and expected to do it unquestioningly. Unfortunately, such disrespect does not teach our children to think about showing respect for others.

The art of disagreeing respectfully and expressing or accepting constructive criticism is declining. We tend to maintain defensive stances and deny feelings. Since children learn most easily from what they see, parents need to make a conscious effort to act in ways that develop trust.

All people have mood swings. Parents can't always respond the same way to opening a teen's bedroom door and discovering the housekeeping disaster within. But if parents pitch a fit one time and look skyward the next, expectations are unclear. Consistency is key in the development of trust. And mistakes, which everyone makes, can be a real learning opportunity if they are dealt with in an honest, realistic manner.

For instance, a friend of your child has just chosen to leave your house earlier than expected soon after disagreement over use of a toy. Sitting down with your child, acknowledging his feelings and then exploring the consequences of the incident is a good place to start. Brainstorming other ways he and his friend might have worked things out differently can then be done, either in writing or out loud. Discussing what the results might be if other things were tried and picking which one to try next time there's a disagreement are good ways to pull the experience together. This kind of interaction shows respect for children and the expectation that they can learn healthy methods of interaction. It also promotes trust in adults for guidance.

## Modeling

We've taken a look at some physical, nonverbal means of communication, at some roadblocks to a two-way exchange of ideas and at some ways of leveling with each other. But children aren't born with these skills. So how do they learn to communicate effectively?

One of the best ways children do this is by following our examples. How a parent talks to his or her child will determine how that child talks to others. Parents who yell at their children frequently are likely to have children who yell frequently. The yelling might not be directed at their own parents, especially if the children fear them, but you can almost count on these youngsters to yell at someone.

There are a lot of good ways we can model for our kids. I remember when my child was one year old and just learning to talk. When she'd point at the sink, I'd know she wanted water. So I'd say to her: "Water, please." She'd then repeat it automatically and I'd give her the water. As kids get older, our modeling needs to change to suit the youngsters' level of communication, but setting concrete examples is still very effective. When my daughter was a preschooler and wanted something in the grocery store, I'd say: "When someone wants candy in the store, whining doesn't make me want to get it. I don't like that tone of voice. I like them to say, 'Mom, may I please have some candy?' " This accomplishes two things: It sets a boundary on behavior I don't want and it models what I do want. The technique has worked effectively with my own children, and with lots of others in school, social and recreational settings.

Many parents set all kinds of boundaries for their kids by saying: "No, don't do that ... don't touch that ... no, no, no."

They're telling their kids what they don't want, but they're not taking the time to say what they do want.

When you set boundaries, they work better if you take the time to tell children *why*. For example, when telling a child not to touch a vase, I explain the history of the object and point out that it is glass and easily breakable. It's a way of showing respect and sharing knowledge. It's also a way of modeling for your children how to explain what they do or don't do.

My younger daughter, Angela, regularly demonstrated as early as age two how much she was absorbing and remembering about the "behavioral boundaries" in our house and the explanations behind them. She would hound her sister with, "You can't jump on the bed. Mom says you might fall and hurt your head," and so on. My older daughter, Amanda, and I wrote a story about her called the "Mini-Mom-Monster." We didn't do anything with the story. I thought it might hurt Angela's feelings and lead to name-calling; but her accuracy continually amazed me.

Until kids are seven or eight, they generally "are" whatever they see modeled. Whenever my kids seem to start acting differently than they have been, I always ask them who else acts like that. They usually have an answer. Then we talk about how that particular behavior affects me and is likely to affect others. I then model what kind of behavior I prefer.

Parents need to remember that learning is a process. Children don't learn many things the first time they hear them. (Exception: loud profanity. It's almost inevitable that kids will imitate that right away!) You have the power of example to teach your children ways to communicate.

Another important aspect of modeling is giving children the verbal tools and understanding to express emotion. When you see a dramatic situation either in real life or on TV, say to your kids:

"What do you think he's feeling?" Or, "I think she's feeling sad right now, because the other kids are teasing her." This kind of discussion can help kids gain insight into the feelings of others and develop a sense of responsibility to the community. But beware: These kinds of discussions can dredge up some sticky situations.

What do you say, for example, if your son or daughter asks you: "Did you try drugs when you were a teenager?" Maintaining a balance between the amount of truth we share and knowledge that our behavior can be a powerful model for our kids obviously can become complicated. If you paint your own youth as mistake-free, your kids will either be skeptical or find your image something overwhelming to live up to. On the other hand, if you share that you frequently stayed out overnight without permission, tried every drug on the shelf and basically did whatever you wanted — your kids might use knowledge of your behavior as justification for similar mistakes.

Youth can benefit from knowing that we all made some mistakes when we were growing up, and what we learned from those errors. However, it's appropriate to modify or limit what we share by asking ourselves two questions:

- Considering the age and maturity of my child, how appropriate is what I'm going to share?
- Do I need to limit what I share or reduce the seriousness of what I did to avoid presenting harmful negative examples?

Just as a parent sometimes classifies a child's scribbles as "very interesting" to avoid discouraging an interest in learning to draw, the best interests of children must be carefully considered before sharing unhealthy choices made in the distant past.

Children might not always choose their parents' way of talking or acting; but with consistent modeling, kids at least will know what their parents think is healthy, responsible and respectful. Two-way communication is critical in enabling children to form a positive self-concept.

# ~ *Chapter Two* ~

# **Expectations**

W hen I was in college, I read about an experiment conducted in Chicago with a group of pre-kindergarten students. All were tested for placement in classes. Then the students were divided into two groups. One group was considered to be of low to average intelligence, entering school without a tremendous number of skills. The other group showed higher intelligence and already possessed good skill levels. When the two groups were assigned teachers, an enormous switch was made. The results of that switch have stayed with me ever since I read about it. And nothing in research or my own life experiences since then has done anything but reinforce the remarkable power of expectations.

In the Chicago experiment, researchers told the teacher assigned to the students who had performed higher on the pretest that the group was somewhat slow. They felt they could do well, the teacher was told, but don't expect too much. The teacher of the group that had scored lower on the test was told that these students were very bright. They might have a little difficulty understanding things at first, the teacher was told, but expect them to do very well.

Now, I have some questions about the morality of doing this to these kids. But the results of the study were certainly profound. When the two groups were tested at the end of the year, their scores almost were reversed. Few studies or case histories illustrate so dramatically the tremendous impact of expectations — from society and from parents — upon how well our children do.

My own experience in both recreational and educational settings has reinforced my belief that we must give kids the benefit of a doubt and let them know we have faith in their ability to do well.

## Community Expectations

Before looking specifically at parental expectations, let's consider those imposed on our children by the society they live in. We live in an electronic age. No longer do children's own expectations of life come almost solely from their immediate communities and from their parents.

Kids today are exposed to so much more. No one is isolated as long as there is a TV in the living room. It's well-documented that children average more than twenty hours of viewing each week. The result is an immense influence upon their concept of what life *should* be — what they can have, what they can do and how things can be accomplished.

It's an electronic age in the classroom, too. Even in my daughter's preschool class, two computers were available for playing games, learning math, drawing dinosaurs and matching words. At home and in the arcades, electronic games for all ages have become a major money-maker. The Air Force looks for video-type hand-eye coordination in its prospective fighter pilots. Even some physical sports now have an electronic connection. A friend of my son recently brought over a power pad. By running and jumping on the pad, he controlled a video athlete on the TV screen performing Olympic feats.

These electronic gadgets and games give our children a great deal of pleasure and a fleeting sense of power. But I also feel that this picture window of the world makes youth feel somewhat more vulnerable. It's difficult to watch television without knowing that some children in the world do not have enough food or shelter or that there is fighting going on somewhere or that violent crimes are being committed right in our own communities. Fear in many cases becomes a realistic expectation that's tough to handle, particularly when you're young.

My six-year-old became very emotional and hid her face during a historical TV drama on the civil rights struggle to integrate the schools. Black high school youth were being hit and kicked by other students and by the police. I hadn't known exactly what was coming or I might not have let her watch, but it's very difficult to keep kids from seeing any violence on TV. We used this experience to talk about the struggles many Americans endured to gain rights and about being respectful and fair to others. The discussion enabled her to handle seeing the violence without having nightmares. I hope it also added to her understanding the importance of treating all people with respect.

However, many children today are not so fortunate as to experience hurts of the world only through the media. The contrast between the way many children live and the ideals they see on TV only intensifies their desire for change. Countless children live in poverty. High unemployment, hunger, and lousy conditions at school don't compare well to the *Cosby Show* or *Full House* families. At the other end of the economic spectrum, affluent families in which there is violence, drugs or little time for parental attention don't compare well, either. If parents don't signal expectations that a child will do well in school or go to college or get a good-paying job, it's easy for kids to see making lots of fast money by dealing drugs as a more realistic career expectation. It's typical of youth to not consider that jail or death are also likely to be in the picture — since the down side comes later.

I once heard Sol Gorden, a well-known parent educator, say that the biggest problem among youth today is "wanting immediate gratification." Even teachers dealing with preschoolers have said they find it difficult to compete with the "immediate gratification" of the fast-paced, ever-changing format of *Sesame Street*. The work ethic that led people to perceive rewards as something that comes after working hard over a sustained period of time is not nearly as common in our communities as it used to be.

My son sometimes compares me with parents who don't require their kids to *earn* special privileges or brand name purchases. He tells me that many of his peers get whatever they want just by asking. My son may exaggerate somewhat, but some parents willingly do "give" their kids almost everything they request. That's what the parents saw as the ideal when they were kids, when all these gadgets were not available and their own parents couldn't afford them anyway. Now, as financially able adults, they shower their kids with gifts. I'm afraid this attitude doesn't help prepare youth to deal with the realities of the work world. Besides, economic studies predict that our kids will be the first generation to have less than their parents.

We need to be organizing in our communities to clearly explain and raise the expectations we have for our youth, for everyone — in terms of competence, caring and responsibility.

## Parental Expectations

I strongly believe that the expectations kids have for themselves are virtually dictated by parents' expectations for their children. It's not always easy, however, for parents to project positive expectations to their offspring. Part of the problem is that kids — like all of us — make many mistakes in the learning process. Too often, parents signal that they expect another mistake to follow.

I went through this process when Amanda was about eight. She seemed constantly to be hurting herself — bumping into things or doing risky gymnastic stunts that ended up in disaster. At first I'd comfort her and ask what I could do. But after a while, her repeated accidents started to make me angry. We talked about how she needed to be more responsible for her own body's welfare, but that didn't seem to help. I found myself always saying to her, "Be careful about this, be careful about that, be careful, be careful, be careful." What this did was send the expectation that she was going to hurt herself again.

In time, I caught myself and thought: "Wait a minute. I need to start expecting her to do OK. To do that, I need to stop telling her every other minute to be careful." So I deliberately changed my behavior. I can't be sure it was this change that made the difference. Sometimes youngsters just go through phases in their physical development where they tend to be more clumsy. But when I stopped nagging her, she did become more careful about what she did. She still had her little disasters, but much less often. It's been quite a relief.

The foregoing example might not seem like a very serious situation to parents of a teenager who is flunking out of school or has stolen money from them, but I do think the principle holds: *Children tend to meet your expectations.* And the percentages are likely to rise if the behavior you want is reinforced in healthy ways and children are allowed a reasonable chance to experience the consequences of mistakes. Our kids need to feel their parents' support and trust in their ability to improve after a mistake. (Specific examples of how to do this will be included in Chapter Four on developing competence.)

It's not easy, but I want to emphasize how useful it is for parents to stop themselves and make sure that their verbal and nonverbal messages project positive expectations. "I know you're going to do a good job on this" can mean a lot when you're transmitting confidence to your child. It becomes a part of them. However, if you follow such a statement with an action that contradicts what you've said, the benefits of your words may well be lost. For example, if you give a compliment on doing the dishes, don't proceed to point out plates that need rewashing.

Two other things parents need to remember in this context: Kids tend to be very sensitive to dishonesty, which they find demeaning; and stereotyping isn't useful.

If we honestly don't have positive expectations in a particular situation, it's probably best to say something like, "I think with hard work, you can do a good job on this" — something you can say sincerely. If you don't have enough confidence in your child's ability to change to say something like this, it's better not to comment at all.

Stereotyping, even if positive, doesn't tend to be healthy for children. A child classified as "Mommy's angel" is likely to have a difficult time dealing with the inevitable "mistakes" made in the growing process and may feel frustrated or shamed by inability to meet the generalized expectation. On the other hand, the child that has been repeatedly told that he or she is the "pain" or "troublemaker" in the family already has two strikes before getting up to bat. Separating specific behavior from the character of the whole child works much more effectively. "I expect to be asked politely when someone wants me to do a favor for them." This kind of statement makes expectations clear without judging the impolite person as "good" or "bad" generally.

## Different Ages, Different Expectations

Communicating positive expectations to our children is tough work at any age. It's made tougher because as your child develops, you must develop new expectations.

In the programs I supervise for teen mothers, almost every day. I hear about parents whose expectations are not age-appropriate for their children. Teen mothers will complain that their child awakened them in the middle of the night and kept them awake, crying and demanding attention. The teen moms talk as if the baby were spoiled and deliberately antagonizing them. Often, the child they're talking about is a month or two old. Similar results prevail when we ask teens at what age their children will be able to accomplish certain tasks or have a particular level of understanding.

Yet, I think even for more mature parents, it's easy to have inappropriate expectations — to fail in understanding what the youngster is capable of doing or making decisions about. It's easy to forget that even though we might wish otherwise, it's not developmentally realistic to expect children to share politely with others until they reach the age of four or five. Similarly, it's important to recognize that when a five-year-old says something happened last week, and it really happened yesterday, he or she isn't lying. The concept of time is not yet understood.

As our children get older, having realistic expectations becomes even more complicated. Even though children have expanded verbal capacities and certainly possess greater conceptual capabilities, they aren't little adults. They still need to be guided through the learning process.

Expecting a fourth-grader to do a report on his or her own with no spelling mistakes or sentence fragments is not realistic in most cases. Expecting teenagers to keep their rooms clean or not be concerned with the impressions they are making on their peers are also unrealistic entries on the parental wish list.

However, parents need to explain to youth on a regular basis what they do expect and the likely consequences of various actions. For instance, when kids hear others teasing it may seem like the appropriate thing to do. They join in the fun. Children will never understand the kind of hurt this behavior can cause unless parents take the responsibility for explaining it.

Our society as a whole also presents youth with numerous inappropriate and mixed expectations. Some of our institutions still expect three- to five-year-old children to sit immobile in chairs for extended periods of time. Those who can't do so are sometimes classified as "hyperkinetic" or "immature." Some fourth-graders are given four to six hours of homework on a regular basis and have almost no time for play. Violence is glamorized and prevalent in the media, yet children are suspended from school for fighting. Being sexually provocative is often projected as necessary for being attractive or "in" among teens, but teen pregnancy and AIDS are serious concerns in our communities.

As parents, we need to be advocates for our children and must try to encourage community institutions to set realistic and developmentally appropriate expectations. We also need to help our children differentiate between what kinds of behavior are appropriate and what kinds are not in creating healthy communities.

Numerous books have been devoted to developmental stages in guiding parents and others who work with youth to an understanding of what is appropriate to expect. I recommend that all parents read at least one book that is specific to the ages of their children. (Some titles will be included in the bibliography.)

The following sections highlight some of the situations that arise at certain ages, illustrating the relationship between the developmental process and parental expectations.

### Babies, Toddlers and Preschoolers

Your family is invited to your niece's graduation. Just after the opening prayer has begun, your two-year-old starts screaming because he wants to get off your lap. What parent hasn't experienced a situation in which Mom or Dad wanted a young child to be quiet and sit still? That doesn't alter the fact that movement and noise are almost synonymous with this age group.

Yet, how many times have you seen parents deal with such age-appropriate behavior harshly — both verbally and physically? Parents attempt to avoid their own embarrassment or the disruption of an event by forcing inappropriate expectations on their children. Often, kids try to mind, but it's just impossible for them to sit quietly through a long ceremony. Their attention span is too short; and their natural urge is to wiggle, talk and investigate — unless they're asleep.

Parents can only balance on that tightrope and consider some possibilities for minimizing difficulties:

- Avoid, whenever possible, putting toddlers into situations that demand holding still and being quiet.
- If the situation is unavoidable, bring quiet playthings or food along to interest and distract children.
- Be prepared to take children out of the area periodically to give them a break.
- Model and encourage "ideal" behavior, but don't punish or become upset if your child can't follow through.

A second issue that comes up with almost every young child is sharing. Parents want their kids to share with their playmates. However, most child-development experts agree that it's not appropriate to expect full understanding of the sharing concept until a child is five or six years old.

That's not to say that parents can't encourage sharing. Even toddlers can feel the warmth of a parent saying thank you to them, after they've offered a lick of their sticky sucker. Modeling how to share with other children helps give them the language they need to share. "Would you like to offer your friend a cookie? It's nice when people share. If you let your friend play with your ball, maybe she will give you the pail and shovel." Encouraging sharing is wonderful, but punishing young children if they don't share is inappropriate. Kids at this age have only relatively recently begun to understand the concept of being independent beings, let alone the idea of ownership. The leap to grasping the benefits of giving up what you just obtained is too much to expect.

A third issue that stands out in my mind with this age group is exploration. We want our children to explore because exploring is how children learn. Kids have a natural curiosity. If we deter it, we hinder their development and they don't gain as much knowledge. Parents sometimes put up blockades to exploration by saying, "Don't touch anything" or "Don't go anywhere" or "Don't take that apart." If a child actually stops reaching out, it may stifle social interaction and creativity.

Child-proofing your house is a good first step in balancing this parent challenge. That way, exploration can proceed without being dangerous to your child or to your good china. Expecting your child to investigate, to take things apart, to taste things and to explore each new thing he or she encounters in a variety of ways can help prevent much parental anxiety.

## Middle Years

Probably the most important concept to remember during middle-year development is the tremendous variation in behavior each youngster will exhibit. I once heard the relationship between this group and their parents compared to that of a yo-yo leaving and coming back to someone's hand. Kids in this age group are flexing the muscles of their fairly new independence at school and in their neighborhoods.

One of the best examples of this for me involved my own daughter. She occasionally would push to spend the night with elementary school friends. I sometimes let her do so; but when she'd come back I'd notice that she really wanted my full attention and we'd have to bond again by spending time together. It's still a little hard for her to be apart for a significant amount of time. She wants to pull away and explore her independence, but then she feels the need for the closeness of her parents. If I can't give her time on her return, she gets a bit upset with me.

During the elementary years there is continuous experimentation with behavior and relationships. I think one of the best things parents can do is to go to the library and get out the old but very relevant Mrs. Piggle Wiggle series and read them with your children. *Mrs. Piggle Wiggle* had a handle on how to raise children's self-esteem long before it became a popular term among psychologists, social workers and teachers. The elementary school-aged children in these books experiment with many of the most common annoying behaviors that try parents to their wits' end. Mrs. Piggle Wiggle has a "cure" for every one of them: The Crybaby Cure, The Selfish Cure, The Careless Cure, The Bully Cure, The Slow Poke Cure, and so on. And although Mrs. Piggle Wiggle uses magic powders and potions, she also signals an expectation that these methods are going to work.

Each cure allows the child to experience either the opposite or the extreme of his or her behavior. This enables them to feel the full impact of what their behavior is causing. They then decide voluntarily either to adopt the new behavior they've had the opportunity to try, or to change the extreme behavior. During the process, each child is dealt with respectfully and it's obvious that protecting the child's welfare is the primary goal.

It's too bad that we don't all have a Mrs. Piggle Wiggle in our neighborhoods, because I'm sure there's no parent who doesn't feel the need for a magic potion every now and then. Since we don't, both my children and I found these books delightful. Whenever my kids show any signs of developing one of the bad habits, referring to what happened in the books helps stop the behavior.

## Teen Expectations

When their sons and daughters are teens, it becomes particularly difficult for many parents to project positive expectations. During this time of transition, parents themselves need to learn to *expect* that their values may at times be very different from those of their teens. Almost all teens also go through periods in which they seem unmotivated or motivated in negative directions, something that is never easy to handle.

However, if parents gain insight into the developmental tasks that teens must accomplish in the struggle to reach maturity, the process can be less explosive.

Bruce Baldwin, Ph.D, identifies six interrelated tasks in *The Struggle for Personal Maturity in Young Adults.* Youth behavior may fall anywhere along each continuum as they seek to accomplish each developmental task. The tasks and their continuums are:

- Resolving the parent-child relationship — becoming emotionally independent vs. remaining childlike and dependent.

> Pseudoindependent,        Personal/Emotional
> Overdependent   ◄•••►   Autonomy

- Solidifying a sexual identity — developing mature ways to feel good about oneself as a man or a woman.

> Hypersexuality,        Personal Adequacy
> Male or Female  ◄•••►   Insecurity as
>                        Male or Female

- Developing personal values — developing a value system that is one's own.

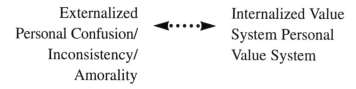

| Externalized Personal Confusion/ Inconsistency/ Amorality | | Internalized Value System Personal Value System |

- Developing a capacity for true intimacy — becoming able to trust and tolerate vulnerability in relationships.

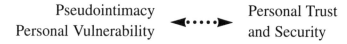

| Pseudointimacy Personal Vulnerability | | Personal Trust and Security |

- The reconciliation of authority — rebellion or submission vs. compromising/negotiation; give and take.

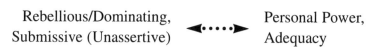

| Rebellious/Dominating, Submissive (Unassertive) | | Personal Power, Adequacy |

- Achieving reasonable self-discipline — balancing impulsiveness and immediate gratification with ability to delay gratification when appropriate.

| Achievement Oriented, Discipline | | Reasonable Self-Pleasure Oriented |

If parents hope to support youth in successfully accomplishing these developmental tasks, the emphasis needs to be on flexibility. I seldom work with a group of teens who don't agree that conflict with their parents primarily revolves around issues of power and control. When offering guidance to teens, we can:

- Expect respect from them, as much as we give respect to them.

- Expect them to have creative options to offer in problem solving.
- Expect them to be involved in the decision-making process.
- Expect them to accept responsibility for handling the consequences of the choices they make.

When parents assert this kind of confidence in youth, it makes it more likely that our teens will become healthy adults.

However, parents need to keep in mind that seldom do teens accomplish these tasks without experiencing crisis or major conflict in one or more of these areas. And in difficult times, we shouldn't hesitate to get help or support from others — for ourselves, for our teens or for both. Constructive suggestions may be considered more seriously by teens if they come from a peer's parent, a neighbor, or a relative not in the nuclear family. It's also sometimes comforting to remember that time inevitably changes people and relationships. Many young people in their twenties adopt the healthy values that their parents taught them before they rebelled as teens. So keep those positive expectations and positive actions flowing.

## A Comfortable Atmosphere

It's so easy for parents, teachers or anyone who works with youth to say they want the youngsters to do well. But intentions aren't really what's important — results are. I can't repeat too many times or emphasize enough just how critical it is to have positive, appropriate expectations of our children, if we want them to be the best that they can be.

As discussed in Chapter One, for communication to happen, there must be an exchange. The bottom line is that each person has a choice of whether or not to participate. The atmosphere we create in our homes by expressing our expectations both verbally and nonverbally determines to a great extent the tone and openness of interactions.

Negative expectations do not establish a comfortable atmosphere for discussion. I believe the sarcasm we often hear from rebelling teens is an exaggerated form of what they've seen adults model in expressing negative expectations for youth.

So try to remember:

- Express positive expectations for your child on a regular basis.
- Consider carefully whether your expectations are age-appropriate.
- Believe in those positive expectations yourself. Children are most likely to meet them when they see we sincerely believe in the expectations.
- Don't generalize from mistakes and thereby create an atmosphere of negative expectations. View them instead as learning opportunities.
- Help promote positive expectations for children in schools and in the community, as well as in your home.

It's easier for children to develop healthy self-esteem when parents have clear, positive expectations.

# ~ *Chapter Three* ~

# Values

**B**eauty lies in the eye of the beholder," like most cliches, often rings true. Take troll dolls, for instance. My older daughter suddenly wanted to bring one to school each week on what her friends called "troll day." Her craving for trolls grew. Before long, my younger daughter also was asking for trolls

I have to admit that at first glance these dolls struck me as downright ugly with their fat, turned-up noses and bulging eyes. Time has mellowed my opinion. Some manufacturers have made trolls appealing enough for me to buy them as presents with my hard-earned cash. Just what made these ugly little dolls so desirable to my daughters? I don't know; but it's important for parents to consider how kids develop their own system of values. And it's important that youngsters grow to understand balancing the value of human interaction with that of materialistic worth.

Some questions to keep in mind as we examine this issue: What encourages us to perceive things one way or another? Why do we attribute more value to certain material goods than others? What determines what we value in relationships with other individuals and with the community as a whole? How do parents inadvertently pass negative values on to their children? How can parents deliberately transmit a healthy understanding of values to their kids?

Once again, one of the most important things for parents to keep in mind is flexibility. By nature, "value" is a relative term and everyone develops his or her own set of values. You can try to jam your own values down a child's throat, but each individual has the power to decide whether to swallow what is offered. Ultimately, parental behavior speaks louder than words in demonstrating values.

## The Basis for Society's Values

As explained by Louis Edward Raths in his book *Values and Teaching,* all societies throughout history have allocated values among their members around the issues of:

- Well-Being: Mental and physical health, security, safety and basic food and shelter.
- Affection: Love and friendship.
- Enlightenment: Information and knowledge.
- Skill: Proficiency.
- Rectitude: Trustworthiness, dependability, responsibility.
- Wealth: Material riches and property.
- Power: Influence over others.
- Respect: Honor, recognition, importance.

Specific values and their expression vary from culture to culture. For example, in some groups power may be concentrated in the hands of a few people. In other groups, power may be widely shared. As individuals are taught the social skills needed to participate in the group, they tend to adopt the value patterns of the group as their own. Thus, the things group members regard as important, the things they need and want, become preferred goals for the individual.

Observe teens at a specific school for a while. Similarities in styles of dress among kids that hang together, or in different "cliques," become obvious. Values will vary within any society, and subcultures will form. What is valued by one community member as very useful may seem worthless to another. Perceptions often vary. As children begin to interact with more people, they need guidance in determining what is healthy in society and what is not.

## Values in Our Society

Parents need to evaluate their own values regularly as a part of helping their children develop value systems. Among the most significant values in any society are those that guide how people are treated in daily life. The importance of these values is illustrated by the *Declaration of Independence:*

> *"We hold these truths to be self-evident, that all men are created equal, that they are endowed by their Creator with certain unalienable Rights, that among these are Life, Liberty and the Pursuit of Happiness. That to secure these rights, Governments are instituted among Men, deriving their just powers from the consent of the governed. That whenever any Form of Government becomes destructive of these ends, it is the Right of the People to alter or to abolish it, and to institute a new Government, laying its foundation on such principles and organizing its power in such form, as to them shall seem most likely to effect their Safety and Happiness."*

In the war for independence that followed this declaration, the slogan "Give me liberty or give me death!" from Patrick Henry's speech was seen by the revolutionaries as a noble and respectable demand. On the other hand, the English perceived these words as an upstart threat to their rightful power. Perception depends on whose interests are being espoused. This particular idea of a revolutionary fight against unjust oppression is, of course, presented with pride in American history books.

Now consider this quote:

*We declare our right on this Earth to be a man, to be a human being, to be respected as a human being, to be given the rights of a human being, in this society, on this Earth, in this day, which we intend to bring into existence by any means necessary."*

Isn't this, too, a basic cry for human dignity? Yet this quote from Malcolm X is still perceived by many in this country as a dangerous threat to our society. Is Malcolm X's goal of respect significantly different from the goals that drove our country's founders? Or is it just that people often have very different perceptions and aren't ready to accept that every human being has the right to the same respect and dignity each of us wants for ourselves? Parents need to ask themselves this question in dealing with everything from interaction with neighbors to dynamics in the school Parent-Teacher Organization to their own children and teens. Too commonly community members ignore negative situations. Sometimes this leads to conflicts escalating and becoming violent.

Gender also influences our society's values regarding the treatment of others. Making assumptions about people and designating roles for them based on gender is commonplace. The profound difference between the value placed on males versus the value placed on females is measured by our economic system on a daily basis. Predominantly female fields just don't pay what "men's jobs" do. For instance, "Equal Pay in Your Pocketbook" (Naomi Barko, *Working Mother,* November 1993, pp. 41-48) documents that the average wages for men and women with comparable education vary tremendously:

|  | High School | College | Master's |
|---|---|---|---|
| Men | $26,218 | $39,894 | $47,002 |
| Women | $18,042 | $27,654 | $33,122 |

Considering such powerful economic influences, parents need to become advocates for our children, so they understand their right to be valued and respected members of our society.

One of the best indicators of a society's general values are the public media — principally television, newspapers and radio. In fact, the media significantly *influence* society's values. Just ask any public relations or advertising executives. My daughters probably wouldn't like trolls if they hadn't been advertised on television. Since the media are of such major significance in our society, we need to be very conscious of our children's exposure to the messages.

Our society sends particularly confusing messages to children — and adults — on a number of topics. There is no way of quantifying the enormous difficulties caused by this mind-boggling confusion of values. Examining some basic ways of sharing healthy values with our children can help to sort out this confusion. (Strategies for coping with the implications of these values can be found in Part Two on handling high stress situations.)

## The Throwaway Mentality

The scarcity of landfill space, even though we maintain the largest dumps in the world, is just one indication of our attitude that everything is available in infinite quantity — use things once, then throw them away. Recycling advocates have made some progress in changing this mentality, but there is still a long way to go.

Unfortunately, this throwaway attitude doesn't stop with material goods. Some of our children are dealt with in the same way. Parents often give up too easily on kids who have problems, and then society frequently writes them off as well. The large number of children permanently in the foster-care system is appalling. Throwaway kids often have very low self-esteem and end up being warehoused at tremendous cost in prisons or mental hospitals. Money is limited for prevention programs that encourage development of healthy parenting or youth programs that teach problem solving and social skills. Minimum effort has been made to prevent the waste of our most precious resource, human beings.

## Alcohol and Other Drugs

The messages youth receive about drugs would confuse Solomon, even if Solomon knew anything about crack cocaine. "Just Say No" plays against thousands of commercial slogans such as: "Headache pain, take aspirin"; "stomach pain, take antacid". Alcohol and tobacco use is portrayed as cool, adult behavior. Yet, when our children get caught with drugs or face problems reflecting in part parental use, society pretends its value system didn't contribute.

The current push in my state is to confine drug prevention efforts to giving youth the "facts." Financial cutbacks are being considered for programs that focus on building self-esteem, problem solving, decision making and other life skills that might really make a difference in helping children avoid drug use.

Elementary students have demonstrated heightened knowledge about the negative effects of using tobacco products. However, numerous older students still choose to smoke. Healthy choices are more likely to be made by children who know they are valued, feel good about themselves and have had basic training in how to assert themselves and deflect negative influences.

## Sexuality

Similar problems arise around this country's schizoid values regarding human sexuality. Recently, I discussed problem solving with a group of high school students in an alternative school. The issue of sex was brought up. Several young men said that getting enough sex was a problem for them. When I raised the topic of relationships, they stopped me and said that they weren't interested in having relationships, only sex.

I pointed out that I felt it was impossible to be sexually intimate with someone without forming some kind of relationship, even if it was superficial or exploitive. Initially, they disagreed — an attitude that unfortunately seems common in our society. Sex is regularly used to sell products on television, at auto and boat shows and in print media. Scantily clad muscle men and young women with hour glass figures permeate advertising. It's easy for youth to get a distorted view of what sexuality is all about. Analysis and discussion with youngsters can enhance understanding.

Girls and young women, in particular, get mixed messages about their bodies. If your bosom isn't well developed, you're often considered unattractive and not as valuable as girls with larger breasts. Yet, girls with larger bosoms have to beware of clothes that follow the shape of their bodies. If you're perceived as showing off your figure, you're asking for trouble and deserve whatever you get.

The number of teenage mothers is appalling — and nearly equaled by the more appalling number of young men who feel no responsibility for having fathered a child. What a tightrope for our teens to walk! To say nothing of AIDS, which lurks out there offering a slow, painful death to those who are not extremely careful about choosing their sexual partners or who become rape victims.

## Violence

Reports of violent crimes dominate the news. Children in elementary schools sometimes are the assailants, as well as the victims. Parents need to consciously consider what values about the treatment of others are encouraging the rise of violence in our communities.

Numerous television and movie heros use violence as their primary tool against bad guys. Such a concentration on violence as a problem solver, even in cartoons designed for the very young, creates social problems. I've witnessed kids giving each other karate kicks or imitating the violence seen in the media. It's sometimes difficult for youngsters to distinguish between reality and cartoon make-believe. But the excitement of physical conflict is what sells, so the emphasis isn't likely to change without enormous community pressure.

Violence by parents against their children or against one another is still considered acceptable by many people who believe that violence is an effective means of training children or keeping a spouse in line. And violence, as even talk-show addicts know by now, breeds violence.

In the movie *Grand Canyon* a young man explains to a cab driver that he carries a gun because that's how he gets respect. Parents have the power to discourage our society from continuing in that deadly direction. If violence is not modeled and youth are trained in alternative methods of problem solving, society will begin to change in healthier directions. Violence needs to be seen as the last resort in defense of our country and of ourselves. Our children need to learn a variety of ways to ensure their own respect without use of violence.

Our message needs to be consistent. When parents hit children in an effort to teach them not to hit others, it is sadly ironic and the most confusing of signals. Parents can provide a model for their children in learning other ways to handle difficulties through discussion and using nonviolent techniques. For example, when one child kicks a playmate, I firmly explain that kicking is not all right. I then find out if there is a problem over something in particular and help them explore other methods of taking care of the conflict. (Specifics of problem solving are included in Chapter Four.)

## Intolerance of Differences

The last value that I'd like to address, one which promotes major problems in our society, is intolerance of differences. People tend to be critical of others whose customs or appearances differ significantly from the majority community. It's interesting that in a society historically built up by people from so many different cultures, that a pressure toward sameness has arisen rather than an appreciation of differences.

Even in communities in which there is general uniformity in terms of skin color, economic status and religion, teasing or gossiping occurs about anyone who is different — not only among youth, but among many adults. Acceptance of oneself and one's confidence level may well be factors in this tendency. (How parents can help stop this trend will be discussed in Chapter Five.)

## Valuing Ourselves

My experience with both parents and children has taught me that people who don't value *themselves* have a more difficult time with life in general, and seem to get into more problem situations.

Parents can demonstrate that they value themselves by doing such things as taking care of their physical, social and mental health. They can set appropriate boundaries and expectations for others so as to encourage respect. For instance, if a child answers a question sarcastically, a parent might reply: "That tone of voice sounds disrespectful to me. It's not OK. Please, try answering me again in a different tone of voice." Throughout this book are a variety of handy strategies for parents to use when conflicts arise and suggestions for building a strong support system.

## Valuing Our Children

Since children come into the world with a limited value system — namely, a basic inclination to survive and to be comfortable ("Change my diaper NOW!"), it's up to parents to promote the development of healthy values in their children.

But, who or what defines healthy? Unfortunately, an all-inclusive child care manual isn't delivered along with each baby and there are no money-back warranties. So parents must seek their own sources of guidance.

However, I strongly believe that certain truths about raising kids must be universally recognized if we want wholesome, productive societies.

We need to value our children. It sounds simple, but it is a truth that is violated many times every day. *First, we must show respect for children's bodies and their feelings.* When my youngest daughter was two, she had to be hospitalized for an infection in her neck. She handled the group examinations, getting the IV in her arm and sleeping in a strange place quite well. Then, the morning of her second day, a pediatrician came into the room. My daughter's back was turned to the door as she watched television. With no greeting or warning, this stranger started pushing on the infected gland. The tiny patient was not only startled but frightened, and immediately began screaming. It would have taken this doctor less than thirty seconds to say "hello" and inform my daughter that he needed to examine her neck. This brief show of respect would have saved much time and trauma.

How many times at gatherings have you seen people shaking babies or holding them in the air in an effort to wake them or play with them, although the baby is obviously uncomfortable? Many adults feel they can do anything they want to kids. Adults are bigger and don't stop to consider the negative messages they send. They aren't conscious of a child's right to be treated with respect.

Each child also *deserves the opportunity to feel that he or she can contribute to society in a meaningful way.* For this to be accomplished, children need feedback telling them what they do is valuable. The structure of our communities, however, is not always conducive to promoting positive feedback. Our educational systems, for instance, have become separated from the working world. When young people served as apprentices in various trades, or worked with their parents on farms or at home, the connection between their contribution and its value to the family and society was fairly obvious. Now, a majority of parents work outside the home. Sometimes youngsters know almost nothing about their parents' jobs. Children usually don't feel they contribute to supporting their families in any way. Many of them don't even think they should. Survey any ten teenagers and see what they say.

Some parents basically require only that their youngsters go to school. Unless teachers help youth understand the value of the connection between what they learn in school now and the working world that lies head, it's difficult for kids to understand the point of school work. Our high school drop-out rate — which surpasses 50 percent in some urban schools — in part reflects this failure. Emphasis must be put on the unique contribution each child can make to the community.

Of course, all parents occasionally are going to not value their children as much as would be best. Parents who never fail to acknowledge their children's feelings don't exist, to my knowledge. But, apologizing after mistakes is a real indicator of respect. Parents also can make a genuine effort to have the primary message they send to their children be one of value and respect for their ideas and their ability to do well.

## Basics for Sharing Values

Specifically, parents can encourage healthy values among children by recognizing that:

- For a child to accept values as their own, those beliefs must be freely chosen.
- Choosing can only be done when there is a variety from which to choose.
- Thoughtful value choices can be made only if there is sufficient information and an understanding of the consequences of making particular choices.

Parents can assist in this process by:

- Sharing our thinking aloud with our children when we make value choices.
- Clarifying the step-by-step process of evaluating choices and considering consequences by discussing decisions that others make on television, in the movies or in the community.
- Directly suggesting, in impersonal terms, a variety of values regarding specific decisions children face, then asking for their opinions on what choice would be best and why. For example, a parent might say: "In similar situations, some people ... What do you think might be a good idea?"
- Demonstrating pride and respect for your own values and encouraging children to do the same. If children aren't comfortable with a value choice they've made, they should be encouraged to rethink the choice.

- Encouraging children to act on their value choices. For example, a child sees another child being teased and thinks it's wrong. He or she can consider whether to intervene directly, get an adult involved or invite the person being teased to leave that situation.
- Promoting the budgeting of time and energy in ways that nourish what's valuable to them.
- Helping children understand that along with any growing independence or freedom comes responsibility. For example, a youngster choosing to use a tool that belongs to a parent should learn that with it comes the obligation to put it back in its original place, in an unchanged condition.

Because children see parents as very "powerful" people, it's important not to use verbal intimidation, rewards in the form of material things or affection, or physical punishment to influence children as they learn the process of valuing. A false sense of value can develop that relies predominantly on external reinforcement.

Value systems evolve over a lifetime. But, by guiding our children through the process of sorting out what's important in life for the individual and to the community, parents can help prevent confusion and irrational decisions. A clear value system can give direction to life and encourage children to act in ways that are positive, purposeful and enthusiastic.

Children are the most precious of our precious human resources. What values our children learn will, to a great extent, determine how we grow as a society. Will it be one that leans more toward coldness or compassion, prejudice or tolerance, ignorance or knowledge, war or peace, hate or love? Parents hold much of the balance of power.

# ~ *Chapter Four* ~

# Competence and Problem Solving

Anthropologist Margaret Mead studied island tribes living in somewhat isolated locations. Her first study was of adolescents on the island Tau in Samoa. The children there generally played half the day and worked half the day. Gradually, they were taught the skills necessary to participate effectively in their society. By the time they were young teens, they were competent in such tasks as taking care of children, obtaining and preparing food, building shelter, and so forth. The transition to choosing a mate and moving into full adult responsibilities seemed to be made easily and the adult community appeared healthy and happy.

Manus, one of the Admirality Islands north of New Guinea, was studied next. In contrast, children and even young teens in this society had no work responsibilities. They played all day and were totally taken care of by the adult community. When old enough to marry, a young man's parents chose a bride for him. The groom then had to borrow the money from his father to pay for his bride. Afterward, he had to spend a great deal of time repaying this debt. Mead noted that adults in this society seemed frequently resentful, unhappy and frustrated. In addition, young couples did not have the life skills necessary to adequately meet each others' needs.

Examination of these two societies points to the importance of encouraging the development of competence in our children. It is difficult for youth to feel positive about themselves if they do not perceive themselves as capable human beings. So how can parents promote competence in their children?

## Flexibility

Flexibility is again a key. Even though books about developmental stages can give parents some idea about what is appropriate to expect from our children, there are no absolutes about when or how long it will take a child to acquire a specific skill.

There is also a significant variation in *how* each child learns best. Some children tend to be audio focused and pick up things well from *hearing* them explained. Others need to *see* something to get a clear understanding. Actively *manipulating objects* may be the optimal learning experience for others. Parents need to experiment with a variety of learning tools in various situations in order to analyze what methods work well for each child. What technique works may also vary according to the particular task. It's another real balancing act.

## Taking Risks

Promoting competency always involves some risk. Do I really want to let her crack that egg? Should I let him pour his own juice this time? Can I bear to watch her hang upside down by her knees for the first time? Risks are involved for both parents and children as new skills are attempted. How parents react to the inevitable mistakes involved in the learning process will significantly influence competency development. Patience is definitely a virtue.

For example, if a child gets most of the egg shell into the pancake or spills juice on the floor, many parents may have a natural urge to yell or be angry. Even the most skilled parent will do so occasionally. But, if we make anger and yelling a pattern, it will discourage children from trying new tasks — the only way children can learn to be competent.

Parents can deal with mistakes in a healthy way. For instance, if a spill occurs have the child become involved in the cleanup. Then suggest, in impersonal terms, some specific techniques that might be more productive.

"Get the rag and the bucket and let's clean up the juice. It sometimes helps if a person asks someone to hold the glass for him, when he's first learning to pour juice. It might be good to take plastic dishes into the tub tonight and practice pouring some more there. Would you like to do that?"

This type of reaction begins to establish a basis for understanding the connection between being able to "do things yourself" and the responsibility that goes with it.

As children grow older, it seems to become even more difficult for parents to have patience with the trial and error and inevitable mistakes in learning new skills. Our expectations often grow faster than our children. But this doesn't mean that learning has ceased to be a process. Only the simplest tasks are done perfectly the first time. And whenever youth take the risk of trying a new task, at least a bit of their self-esteem is on the line — parents must handle the situation with care.

## Keeping the Process Going

We need to keep in mind that children become frustrated and sometimes angry with themselves when they can't do something right away. What parent hasn't seen a toddler — or an eleven-year-old, for that matter — have a tantrum when the child couldn't immediately accomplish something he or she wanted to do? Such situations can be used as an opportunity to teach methods of handling uncomfortable feelings and to teach persistence.

For example, what if a child wants to tie a shoe, but can't? Respecting and acknowledging the child's feelings, rather than denying the problem, usually is an effective first step. Suggestions can then be made impersonally about methods of simplifying the task or offers made to help. "Some people find it easier to learn to tie shoes if they have two different colors of strings pulled through the top of a shoebox. Would you like to try that?" Or, "Making bows was hard for me to learn to do, too. Would you like me to work with you for a few minutes?"

Part of respecting your child is being willing to accept "no," if the child doesn't want to attempt the new task. Ask children what they think would make the task easier for them. Encouraging them to contribute to the problem solving sometimes works well, too. But sometimes, putting the task aside for a while and redirecting attention elsewhere is the best strategy.

"You've been working awfully hard on that puzzle for a long time. Let's take a break together and get a fresh start on it after lunch."

"I know you're very busy putting that plane together, but could you help me over here for a minute?"

It's not uncommon for children to try so hard that they incapacitate themselves. When they get back to a task after a break, it frequently seems less difficult.

## Projecting a Positive Attitude

More often than not, when children are learning to walk, adults are very encouraging.

"Oh look, you took a step! Come to me. Oops, down you go. Well, get up and try again! Come on, you can do it!"

Seldom do you hear parents say to a toddler: "You fell down! Now, why did you do that? You better get it right the next time. I just don't understand why you can't do better. You should try harder!"

Few other childhood learning experiences garner such near-universal patience, support and positive expectation from adults. In fact, our culture in general does not look kindly on mistakes or show patience with youth who don't meet their expectations — whether the expectations are appropriate or not. This "quick to judge" attitude tends to create defensiveness and discourage motivation.

When older children are learning new skills, parents often seem to forget that encouragement is still one of the most effective ways to support the child, rather than criticism, threats, teasing or directives. Emphasis again needs to be put on positive expectations.

## Our "Natural Impulses"

It's important for parents to keep in mind how they were treated when they were learning new tasks in childhood. Were your parents afraid to let you try things? If you couldn't do something right away, did your parents say, "Just let me do it"? Did your parents do almost everything for you automatically, because of their need to make sure you were well cared for? Did your parents re-do all of your chores, to make them better?

If our parents did these things while we were growing up, it's more likely we'll behave in a similar way with our children. It comes naturally. Parents who behave this way often have good intentions, but none of these dynamics promote development of competence. How would you feel if your boss told you to keep a lid on any new ideas or did everything you'd done over again? Your motivation certainly would suffer.

Again, there's no parent alive who will never make these mistakes. But, we can try to be conscious of messages we're sending to our kids about their ability to learn new things, admit our mistakes and be creative in the ways we encourage competence.

**Problem Solving**

Confidence in one's ability to develop competence can melt like snow in April unless we are able to handle problem situations. For instance, a child comes home from school one day obviously unhappy. Spilling some food at lunchtime turned out to be a laughing matter for the whole class. Dread for the next school day hangs heavy in the air. Teasing sometimes makes children feel they are not competent to do anything right. It's not true; but an overwhelming feeling of incompetence takes over for a while. (We'll look at a way to deal with this example in a few pages.)

No one, of course, can go through life without facing numerous problems. Some are little and some are big. Some must be dealt with immediately and others can be put off a while. Some we cause ourselves and others are totally out of our control. Some involve us directly, and others we only witness from a distance. Some problems cause automatic, reflex-type reactions. Others allow us time to plan our reactions. But there is little formal training for either parents or children on handling difficult situations in healthy ways.

How can a parent help his or her children become competent in this crucial skill of problem solving?

Parents can begin to teach problem solving almost as soon as children can talk in sentences. When one child grabs a toy from another, it's an opportunity for parents to begin to explore negotiations with those involved.

"People don't like it when someone grabs something away from them. They like people to ask them nicely if they can have a turn. 'May I please see that red truck,' might be a good way to say it. Try it yourself."

By the time children are four or five years old, brainstorming or thinking of a number of possible ways to handle a situation can be done with a little parental guidance: "What are some ways this problem could be settled without making anyone feel bad?"

After the kids have made their suggestions, parents might wish to add a few more ideas, using impersonal terms. "Sometimes when two people want the same toy at the same time, they agree to set a timer and each take a five-minute turn with the toy. Others figure out a way that they can both play with it together."

In reality, parents here are introducing the steps of an organized problem-solving method that is useful for anyone throughout life:

1. What is the problem?
2. Brainstorm possible solutions.
3. What will happen if I choose each solution?
4. Pick the best option. (I choose "X.")
5. Act. (Do option "X.")
6. How well did it work? Well or not so well?
7. Congratulate yourself or try another option.

These steps may seem cumbersome at first, but the method becomes easier as you use it. Defining a problem carefully and thinking about the results of your actions before you take them can save time, trouble and pain for both parents and children.

## Roadblocks to Problem Solving

Working with children on problem solving often gets sidetracked by three common barriers.

When problems arise, it is difficult if not impossible to solve them with a "crisis mentality." One major characteristic of this type of thinking is tunnel vision or the inability to see a variety of solutions to a problem. Tunnel vision amounts to self-imposed limits on creative solutions.

Even if no crisis exists, our tendency is to do things the way we've done them before. Familiarity makes things feel more comfortable. The healthiest solutions, however, may not always be those that are easiest or most comfortable at first. Flexibility is again of utmost importance.

To help young people become more aware of the importance of flexibility in problem solving, our youth program facilitators ask youngsters to connect nine dots. The directions given are: "You may use only four straight lines to connect the dots. Once you put your pencil down on the paper, you may not lift it again until the connections are complete." Try this exercise yourself for five minutes before you read any further.

• • •
• • •
• • •

Most people cannot find a solution to this puzzle the first time they see it. Why? Because they try to stay within the outline of the box itself, even though no one has said that was necessary. (If you're still puzzled, the solution is at the end of this chapter.)

In problem solving, people also tend to stay within their self-imposed boxes. They don't carefully consider all the options. Parents who break this pattern can help their children do the same.

A second major roadblock is parents' inclination to get into power struggles with their youngsters. The minute sons or daughters sense that parents are trying to "control" the situation, rather than respectfully involve them in finding a solution, participation is likely to shut down.

Yes, parents have had more life experience. Yes, they may better understand the consequences of choosing various ways to handle a particular situation. But imposing a solution on children does not further their competence in problem solving. Children need to feel that options they suggest will get genuine consideration.

During brainstorming, it's sometimes useful for parents to suggest options they know wouldn't have good consequences. That way the negative consequences can serve as a model in eliminating poor choices. There are times when parents should not allow certain options to be tried because of safety issues; but persuasion rather than force is always a better technique.

A third major roadblock to problem solving is a *judgmental attitude.* Parents need positive expectations and two-way communication if they hope to work successfully on a problem with their children. No one likes the feeling of being critically judged. Defensive feelings are magnified if children feel parents are "talking down" to them or "treating them like babies."

### A Problem-Solving Sample

Teasing is a very common problem among school-aged youth. Let's look at a model of how parents could encourage a child to use the problem-solving steps for the example about spilled food.

**Step 1.** Defining a problem is not always as easy as it seems. Often, what seems obvious on the surface is not always the real problem. Insecurity and power struggles — between child and parent, or between child and peer — are common underlying issues. Children being made fun of at school unfortunately happens too often. A problem-solving conversation might begin:

"Can you tell me more about what happened at school?" (After a child shares an experience, it's useful to let him or her know that you were listening carefully by paraphrasing what was said or expressing empathy before getting into exploring solutions.)

"It sounds like it really felt awful to have that kind of accident. Nothing can really be done about the food spilling, but let's take a look at what can be done about facing school tomorrow." (Then define the problem more specifically.) "Is it the embarrassment or teasing that bothers you more? Have you felt uncomfortable with students at other times or is this the first time you've felt so bad?" (Part of defining the problem is finding if a child has a general feeling of insecurity with other students.)

It's important for parents to keep in mind that youngsters have a choice in whether or not they share anything with you about what happened, so try to avoid setting up roadblocks.

**Step 2.** Brainstorming must center on what the actual problem turned out to be. In some cases, brainstorming might need to be done on a couple of different issues. "What could you do tomorrow, if kids start teasing you again?" (Parents might need to make the first suggestion to get things started or suggest additional ideas for the child to consider. Be sure to keep in mind that during brainstorming, there is no evaluation of the ideas.)

A list might include:

- Pretend you're sick and leave school.
- Be silent, but say to yourself, "I know I'm OK!"
- Firmly tell the teaser to leave you alone.
- Say they might be right.
- Hit the person doing the teasing.
- Tease the other person back.
- Cry when you're teased.
- Mobilize other kids to support you.

**Step 3.** In evaluating what you've brainstormed, parents can encourage children to thoroughly discuss what is likely to happen if he or she picks each suggestion. Consideration should be given not only to the consequences for the child, but to the impact on others.

**Step 4.** The child should choose what solution to try and make preparations for taking action. In the case of teasing, a parent might want to role play the next day's scene so the child can actually practice what he or she wants to say.

If a child decides to try what parents might consider a bad choice, they need to ask themselves: "Is anyone's safety threatened by this choice?" If not, don't interfere any more than to make sure that the likely consequences have been considered.

It's better for children to experience making poor choices when they're young. It will provide a useful lesson for later reference, when bad choices might have more serious consequences.

Boundaries must be explained more thoroughly if unsafe options are being given serious consideration. Children need to know specifically, for instance, that it is not OK to hit or kick others. Brainstorming additional safe alternatives is useful in this limit-setting process.

**Step 5.** Sometimes children come up with good ways of dealing with a problem, but have difficulty actually taking action. Encouragement can be effective in building confidence. Let your child know that you are pleased a choice has been made and that he or she is taking responsibility for doing something about the problem. Gaining a sense of having some control in dealing with difficulties is often half the battle. On the other hand, using high-pressure tactics or ultimatums usually lower self-confidence and discourages action.

**Step 6.** After an option has been tried, parents can help youngsters evaluate its effectiveness. If an option did not work very well, the conversation is often more difficult. Youngsters might tend to be defensive. Careful listening and using tentifiers as you show empathy can encourage healthy two-way communication. An atmosphere of interrogation or an I-told-you-so judgmental attitude discourages further interaction.

**Step 7.** When giving congratulations because an option worked well, it's good for parents to emphasize how important it is that a conscious method was used for problem solving. If the option chosen didn't work well, it helps to concentrate on letting children evaluate why it didn't work and what other possibilities can be tried.

Actively involving children in problem solving not only assists in changing that particular situation, but helps them recognize the usefulness of this process as a skill throughout life. Discussion with children about flexibility in trying options and the fact that no one method works all the time can reinforce the value of going through this process.

Helping children establish healthy patterns for developing competency and problem solving is one of the greatest legacies a parent can pass on to a child.

*~ The Parenting Tightrope ~*

# ~ *Chapter Five* ~

# Understanding and Appreciating Differences

H ow would you like to face a judge and jury and be found guilty on the basis of "evidence" such as skin color, religious preference, cultural background or manner of dress? Impartial judgment, of course, is one of the basic, stated values of our nation. It is, however, an ideal. In practice, even at the end of the twentieth century, some people pass judgment every day against people who are "different."

Our children are not born with undemocratic genes. It is up to us as parents, however, to communicate a value system based on mutual respect. Otherwise, our society will reap the seeds of scenarios like the following one I have encountered in working with children and families:

A five-year-old comes home from school upset one day. She says that the two girls with whom she has been best friends all year have decided not to play with her anymore. When she asked why, the girls told her it was because she was black. One of the girls doing the excluding was of Oriental descent. The other was Jewish.

A white high school student says it's OK to be mean to black people — none of whom he has ever met — because he knows that "they" are mean, too.

"All Mexicans are lazy" is the serious opinion of one rural student, who learned that stereotype from his mother.

A teen mother openly expresses her hate for Arabs. When asked what she might learn by speaking to a visitor from an Arab country, she says, "Nothing," explaining that Arabs don't know anything she'd want to learn.

All of these attitudes were learned, at home or on the street. Even in communities where differences seem minimal on the surface, not many people go through the growing process without experiencing some kind of isolation or threat because they are different from others. The difference might be the cost of the clothes they wear, the shape of their eyes, their religion, the way they talk, a handicap or an unacceptable social habit.

Whatever the reason, the children who are singled out suffer great pain, always mentally and sometimes physically. Left unchecked, intolerance of differences will cause even greater damage to our society than it has already. Within a very few years, the citizens now considered minorities will outnumber the current white majority. Many sectors of the business community have recognized how important it will be for managers to deal with people from a variety of backgrounds. All of us — and we are *all* different — must prepare for a multicultural world.

As I write these words, the creator of the most successful children's story ever told — E.T — has just won an Oscar for *Schindler's List.* That Steven Spielberg found it necessary to remind the world that six million people were massacred in Europe, in our time, because they were *different* is nothing short of amazing. But he was right. Lives are still being lost in struggles for human rights throughout the world today.

One holocaust victim recently explained to me that he willingly shared his experiences in Nazi Germany, even though talking about it always gave him nightmares. He wanted to be sure such incredible intolerance never again exploded into genocide.

The attitudes of soldiers towards Jewish people during World War II and the Vietnamese, during the Vietnam war, allowed them to indiscriminately slaughter thousands of innocent people. Historically, harsh treatment of anyone easily identified as physically different from the "ruling" group has been more easily accepted by society.

In the face of such horror, it may seem at first farfetched to think of parenting as the first step in stopping the tide of bigotry. But the values we teach our children today will significantly influence the direction in which the world goes tomorrow. Hitler understood this very well.

The perceived threat because of numbers also has influenced attitudes and treatment. For instance, discrimination against Mexicans near the southern U.S. border is very common and there is growing resentment of many Americans towards the Arabs and Japanese in communities where there is a significant concentration of immigrants. Resentment is openly expressed towards the financial success many of foreign born have achieved in this country. Are people with these attitudes also critical of Americans who have made fortunes on businesses in other countries? Not likely.

It is an important part of the parental balancing act to promote humanitarian attitudes that tolerate individual beliefs and differences of all kinds. Parents create the first step toward healthier, more peaceful communities.

## The Learning Process

What two-year-old boy hasn't caused a smile by soaping up his face and pretending to shave? And what two-year-old girl hasn't dressed up in her mother's old clothes and paraded around the house?

Children spend most of the first few years of their lives imitating those around them. When toddlers successfully say the same words or act the same as others, frequently they're rewarded. It is through copying that children become comfortable and familiar with whatever their world happens to be, gradually acquiring the skills needed to function in society.

As a child's world broadens, he or she becomes more aware of differences. Every parent has been surprised by a comment their young child made about someone on the street who was handicapped or significantly different in some other way. At this point, parents have a choice about how to guide youthful perspective. How can parents teach healthy respect and an appreciation of what can be learned from the differences between themselves and others?

A good way to start developing a healthy consciousness about similarities and differences with children is to make a game of it. Have a youngster pick another person with whom to compare himself or herself. Make a list of characteristics each of the two has in common, physically, mentally and socially. Then make a similar list of differences.

This kind of analysis leads nicely into discussion of how every person possesses similarities to and differences from the people with whom he or she shares the planet. It's the unique combination of traits in each of us that makes the world such an interesting place.

When children are young, they seem to have a natural curiosity about anything new or different. This presents a prime opportunity for parents to begin sharing a healthy perspective on differences. Show children pictures of people from different cultures. Ask them what they think they might be able to learn from them. Even three- or four-year-olds can come up with such things as learning a different language, how to make something they see in the picture or sharing an unfamiliar food.

With older youth, emphasizing that America historically has been a "melting pot" of people from a variety of racial, ethnic and religious backgrounds can be useful. Kids can informally interview someone over fifty years old about how life was different when they were growing up as another way to encourage a more accepting perspective on differences.

On the street, if not at school, every child is going to see people with physical handicaps. A lack of explanation can cause children to feel uncomfortable. Having children imagine what it would be like not to be able to walk, temporarily, because of a broken leg can provide insight into the difficulties faced in our society by handicapped people. Such discussions further a child's understanding that people with physical handicaps have the same needs as anyone else to be liked, accepted and to have fun. The tone of respect for others in general can also be established during this conversation.

### Generalizations, Harmless Myths and Prejudice

While increasing insight into differences, children can be asked to consider the likelihood of specific statements about people being true.

By discussing distinctions among the categories of statements, children can get in touch with more humane ways of interacting with others.

*Universal generalizations* are statements that almost everyone would agree are true for people, regardless of background. For example:

- Children learn a lot from their parents.
- People like to eat good food.
- People like to be treated with respect.
- Children cry when they get badly hurt.

Considering statements such as these draws attention to the fact that human beings everywhere have certain feelings and habits in common.

Parents can also point out that some generalizations, although not negative, are not true either. For example, if a child assumes all people of Oriental descent use chopsticks, parents can explain such habits often depend on culture, rather than race.

*Prejudice,* on the other hand, includes statements that personify a group of people in a negative way.

- Mexicans are lazy.
- Black people are not as intelligent as whites.
- People with accents are slow thinkers.

These types of beliefs often cause people to deal with others in inhumane ways. By finding out children's reactions to such statements and discussing what they've heard in the community or on TV, parents can encourage children to become more clear about what they believe and why. If examples of prejudice are brought up, parents can encourage youngsters to think about how it would feel if they were discriminated against on the same basis.

Covering a book with plain paper and asking children to guess its content is another good way to promote understanding that looking at the outside of a person doesn't tell you what's inside. Maintaining an open attitude and avoiding lecturing are key in this type of discussion.

## Setting Guidelines for Behavior

Cruel teasing is so prevalent in our society that almost every child is going to "test out" whether or not it's acceptable. However, parents and community institutions together can firmly set guidelines that help children develop more caring attitudes toward others.

Any child can be asked to think about ways they *do not* like others to treat them. Then they can consider how they *do* like to be treated themselves. Such a discussion offers an opportunity for parents and teachers to share their opinions about certain kinds of behavior in a nonjudgmental way. At the end of such a discussion, coming to an agreement about acceptable and unacceptable behavior is ideal. Once these guidelines are established, they can be referenced whenever they are broken. "We've agreed that it doesn't feel good to call each other names. Let's find another way to share what you're feeling."

Language does need to be adjusted to the age of the child. I've found even with teens, however, that it often works to say firmly: "That's not OK. It needs to stop."

When parents and children watch TV together or see others at play, Mom and Dad can discuss with their youngsters how someone might feel in that particular situation. This helps children become more sensitive to the feelings of others.

Letting children know it is *not* OK to make fun of others and that they, too, could at some point be the object of teasing is important. For example, everyone some day will have a pimple on his or her face. Not being perfect is part of being human and we need to have compassion. Teasing someone about a pimple might seem harmless. But it *could* be very hurtful. Role playing with youth is often good preparation for handling teasing situations. Options to practice can include:

- Ignore the teasing and tell yourself something you like about yourself.
- Look the teaser in the eyes and say calmly, "I'm sorry, I didn't hear you," repeatedly until he or she gets bored.
- Give an unemotional response that "you suppose" what they're saying could be true. (If you aren't disagreeing or denying what they're saying, it's not as much "fun" to tease.)
- Discuss the situation with an adult you trust (parent, friend, teacher).
- When the teaser is of the opposite sex, point out that this kind of teasing usually means the person likes you but doesn't know how to tell you so. Thank them for the attention.
- If you're being teased for not doing something you disagree with, don't *just* say "no." Repeat it as many times as it takes, politely and firmly, along with a "rule" you follow in dealing with that subject. For example: "No, I don't want to smoke because I know it hurts my lungs."

Leaving the situation or distracting teasers with another subject are good techniques children can use to avoid taking part in being cruel to others.

In a sixth-grade class I worked with, one youngster was often being teased to the point of tears by four others. When the teasers were confronted, one of them said, "Why didn't anyone ever tell us that we shouldn't tease?" Parents and institutional personnel both need to set down specific guidelines for treatment of others. What may be obvious to us, might not be obvious to youth.

If every child gained a clear understanding that each of us could be targeted by a group of others for harassment, and how that would feel personally, the world would become a kinder place.

## Competitiveness

Among any group of kids, you're likely to hear, "I can do that better than you," or "I'll beat you!" This type of bantering tends to set up situations in which one person is inevitably a "loser."

Competitiveness sometimes becomes emphasized by parents and children to the point where activities are no longer pleasurable themselves, but become primarily a means of proving oneself "better" than others. Other times, people choose not to do their best because they have been taught that doing too well will isolate them from others. Neither of these attitudes is healthy. Sports, academic achievements, artistic performances and social behavior are areas in which parents and other adults commonly overemphasize competition. This can cause undue stress and defensiveness in youth.

How does the question of competitiveness affect understanding and appreciating differences? The battle for oneupmanship can easily reinforce prejudice in our society. It can be very attractive to "losers" in competition with their particular group to defensively treat those of other groups inhumanely. The warped sense of "well, at least I'm better than they are" can be very destructive in our diverse communities.

I prefer to challenge each child to be the best that he or she can be, regardless of the competition. Enjoying what you're doing is emphasized, rather than who wins. With just a little imagination, cooperative activities can be encouraged, too.

Balancing is again the important thing. All children need the experience of not winning, because handling loss or disappointment is inevitably a part of life. They also need to experience success to develop competence. However, we must regularly examine whether or not we are promoting self-motivation and positive self-esteem or creating dependence on external approval.

Each child's temperament varies, but parents need to keep reminding themselves that all learning is a process, not an event. Healthy attitudes will be developed only through repetition and positive modeling over time.

## Building a Community

One of the most significant ideas parents can share with their youngsters is the understanding that each of us individually contributes to creating the atmosphere of the communities in which we live.

The easiest way I have found to share this idea with youngsters is to suggest that they imagine that one of their teachers has been injured in a serious auto accident. We then brainstorm about all the people who are affected by this particular incident. Even three- and four-year-olds can come up with lists of people affected, including firemen, students, ambulance drivers, doctors, family and friends.

We then talk about what responsibilities each person has for helping the situation. Possible consequences if people fail to handle their responsibilities are also considered.

The point is then made that every time someone is hurt, it affects many community members. This is true whether the "hurt" is physical or mental. When a child is picked on by others, he or she is more likely to be mean to other community members. There also is the fear of befriending a victim, to avoid becoming a victim oneself. The community gradually becomes more unsafe for all members. Such discussion seems to effectively raise consciousness that each of us needs to treat others with the same consideration and respect that we want for ourselves.

One teenager I met recently said she thought it was impossible for humankind to change — to learn to live peacefully and respectfully with others. The fact is, however, each can make a positive difference. We have a choice. Parents can model humane treatment of others and teach our children to do likewise. Or we can continue to see hate and violence grow.

*~ The Parenting Tightrope ~*

~ *Chapter Six* ~

# Conflict and Decision Making

C onflict and decision making are invariably connected. Decisions only have to be made when there is more than one option available. The conflict involved may be as simple as internal mixed feelings about what kind of ice cream someone wants or as complicated as trying to decide whom to spend time with when two best friends have had a fight.

And similarly, whenever conflicts between people happen, there are always decisions to make about what to do, how to act or what to avoid.

The skills youngsters have when facing conflict and making decisions will inevitably affect how they view themselves throughout the growing process. By approaching conflict using a variety of techniques, parents can gradually encourage a child to adopt healthy values for making his or her own decisions, rather than relying on outside forces to determine their choices. Thoughtful nonviolent ways of resolving conflict can be learned, as well.

Each child born has the potential to be a positively contributing member of our society. Promoting healthy decision making is a key in creating this as reality.

The mother of a twelve-year-old begins to put some clothes away in her child's dresser drawer. Everything is a crumpled mess. She decides to fold things neatly, as a favor. She is shocked to discover a small plastic bag containing marijuana and some cigarette papers.

A problem, for sure. Just how is she going to deal with this when her child comes home from school?

In such a situation, handling a problem is more complicated because it's likely that parent and child have a conflict of values. It appears this youngster has made a deliberate decision to engage in a harmful and illegal activity. Something like this frequently awakens all kinds of negative emotions in parents: disappointment, sadness, hurt, irritation, anger, anxiety and insecurity.

Many parents may have an almost uncontrollable urge to attack their child verbally or physically. But the question parents need to ask themselves first is: What do we want to accomplish?

Most parents simply want this behavior to stop, now and forever. If so, careful consideration needs to be given to what approach is most likely to work.

Drs. Jordan and Margaret Paul in their book *If You Really Loved Me ...* maintain there are only two ways to deal with conflict.

The first is to protect yourself from fear and pain. This type of response lets us avoid personal responsibility for our own feelings, behavior and resulting consequences. We feel we are victims of others' choices and that they are wrong and we are right. There is a tendency to be:

- Defensive.
- Closed, angry and blaming.
- Uninvolved or withdrawn.
- Judgmental of others.
- Unloving.

It's natural for us to want to protect ourselves, but responding in this way usually ends up creating more pain, rather than relieving it.

The second way to handle conflict, according to the Pauls, is with the *intent to learn*. To accomplish this, we need to be:

- Open to wanting to learn and hear what the other person is really feeling.
- Non-judgmental — not feeling that we are *completely* "right" and the other person *completely* "wrong."
- Respectful of the other person as an important and worthy human being.
- Loving and able to show loving feelings, even though there is conflict over a particular issue.

*Intent* is a key word here. Do our verbal messages, as well as our body language, transmit to the other person what we *really* want to do in a conflict situation? Are we open to discussion and learning or are we not?

Just as in the case of learning any new skill or problem-solving method, it's easy to forget that crashing into a protective, self-defensive mode might not be the best way to deal with conflict. For many of us, this defensive stature is a habit.

It is also frequently natural for parents to assume when conflict arises that their children have caused the problem deliberately. Sometimes, but by no means always, this is true. Children see the world from a different perspective and often haven't had enough life experience to fully understand the implications of their behavior.

So think twice before taking action. If you find marijuana in a child's drawer, what is the purpose of your response? Do you want to make your child defensive by attacking and have him or her clam up tight? Or would you rather have a discussion with the intent of learning the extent of the problem and any underlying pressures that might be encouraging this behavior? Don't you want to share with your child concern for his or her well-being?

Beginning a discussion by non-judgmentally stating, "I found these in your drawer and I'm concerned about your health," frames the issue and the feelings in manner that promote discussion. Be patient in waiting for a response — you want hear from your child, *not* lecture to him or her. Keep in mind, however, approaching a child with the intent to learn doesn't guarantee there will be two-way communication — it only improves the chances.

## Underlying Causes of Conflict

**Behavioral symptoms of other problems:** When conflicts arise, it's of upmost importance for parents to remember that negative behavior doesn't always clearly point to the actual problem.

One morning when my daughter Amanda was six, she just wasn't cooperating as I was getting ready to take her to school before work. She dressed slowly and ate breakfast like a snail. My frenzied requests for her to hurry up seemed only to slow her down. My immediate urge was to get angry and threaten her, if her behavior didn't improve. I decided instead to deal with her with the intent to learn.

I empathized with her not feeling too peppy and then asked if anything was wrong. She said she didn't know exactly why, but she felt kind of mad at me.

The previous evening, I had yelled at her. I'd run to get towels, while giving Amanda's younger sister a bath, asking Amanda to watch over her. I had come running to the sound of cries after baby sister bumped her head in the tub. I asked Amanda why she hadn't done a better job watching her. She said she didn't like that task and wished I wouldn't ask her to do it. I apologized for yelling and explained why I needed her help, even if she didn't want that responsibility. I thought the issue was settled, but evidently it wasn't for her.

When I asked if she was still mad from the night before, she said she thought that could be it. We then took about two minutes to talk again about what had happened and she explained how really frightening it was when her sister got hurt. Afterward, she got ready for school quickly and well.

It took much less time to have that discussion than it would have taken to continue to struggle with her resistant behavior — and it was a lot less frustrating.

In group work with youth, we find over and over again that a variety of negative behaviors have their roots in unresolved losses due to separation of parents or death of loved ones, irritably due to lack of coping skills, or frustration because of other difficult situations. Sometimes it's hard to understand the connection between aggressive behavior toward other kids, not doing school work or inability to follow directions, and the feelings of rejection, anger or helplessness bottled up inside children. Parents often fail to realize that if children have experienced a serious trauma in their lives, they need to rework their perspective on that event as they enter each new developmental stage. Specific support is useful in this process.

Approaching a child with the intent to learn can open up doors to real understanding and an opportunity to problem solve together.

**Conflicting values:** Struggles often arise with youth because of the differences between the values their parents find acceptable and those that encourage acceptance among a child's peers. Whether or not a person feels accepted in a community has a lot to do with his or her self-esteem. Therefore, it is very important to deal with such conflicts thoughtfully.

Research has shown that even though peers influence each other, parental influence continues to be generally more significant — even through the teen years. For example, a 1990 study of sixth- through twelfth- grade, youth by the Search Institute in Minneapolis indicates such factors as "positive family life, parental standards and parent involvement in schooling" are a stronger deterrent to at-risk behavior than "positive peer influence." However, keeping two-way communication flowing is again the challenge. Parents need to carefully choose which issues are worth struggling over. Is it really important whether or not class fashion dictates wearing two different colored socks, or clothes that are three sizes too large?

Differing values over issues that can affect health and safety are the ones that merit our prime attention. The use of alcohol or other drugs, physical challenges or dares that aren't reasonable, and hurtful teasing of others are examples of the kinds of activities youth sometimes feel pressured into participating in to gain acceptance within the group they've chosen as their community.

Open discussions that include looking at consequences and sharing parental life experiences can be useful to broaden children's perspectives. Prevention, rather than reaction to crisis, is generally a better choice whenever possible. Parents need to make a conscious effort to ensure that their children know what their values are and the basis for them. Then, when youth have to make choices, they'll at least be making informed decisions.

**Power struggles:** Read the following work rules, then close your eyes for a minute and imagine how you would feel.

Suppose you worked in a place where:

- The boss always tells you what to do, how to do it and when to have it done.
- You aren't asked for suggestions, and questions about why something is being done aren't appreciated.
- If you talk back or give the boss a hard time, you're given time off with no pay on the grounds of insubordination.
- Scheduling dictates when you can have meals, or even when you can go to the bathroom.

How do you think *you* would feel? When I ask parents this question, they commonly answer that they would feel resentful, frustrated, angry. They say they would feel the need to rebel, sabotage or change jobs. Some parents who actually worked under such circumstances verified that they felt exactly this way.

When households or schools are run similarly, with the parents or teachers taking on an authoritarian, dictatorial role, the same emotions mentioned by parents tend to develop among the kids.

Sometimes conflict arises between youth and their parents even when there isn't any significant difference in values. *Power* is the actual culprit in the conflict. By the age of one, almost every child has begun the task of trying to gain some control over his or her own life. A prime task adolescents need to accomplish in reaching maturity is resolving the question of authority and the ability to act independently. The process of this separation usually involves defensive reactions by both adults and children.

For example, what clothing or hair style a child chooses or the foods they choose to eat could be their way of expressing a need to control certain aspects of their lives. Their choices sometimes set their parents' own hair on end. However, dealing with this conflict with the intent to learn can sometimes help promote discussion about control and limits, rather than the surface issues.

When youth feel they have some degree of power in determining their own destiny, it significantly affects how they feel about themselves and the effort they are willing to put into accomplishment. Although some parents think they'd rather maintain all power in their children's lives until they are at least eighteen years old, the world doesn't work that way. In actuality, this type of control will not allow the growth of skills necessary for children to make healthy choices. The question parents face is how to support and guide their children.

## Helpful Techniques for Dealing with Conflict

No one technique will work in all situations, especially those in which emotions run high. Sometimes taking a few deep breaths when conflict arises gives us a little more energy to face the situation in a more productive way. If parents keep in mind having the "intent to learn" as each of the following methods is used, positive results are more likely.

**Promoting healthy decision making:** A four-year-old named Jimmy is playing next to David, who is driving a red dump truck across the floor. Jimmy decides he wants the truck. Without saying a word, he grabs the truck and gives David a push.

Most parents wouldn't consider this an acceptable way to behave. Jimmy made a choice to take something he wanted without asking and used some physical force in the process.

86

However, after acknowledging that a major portion of parenting will involve encouraging children to make healthy decisions, it's useful for parents to think about what they really consider to be healthy.

As I've watched parents react to situations similar to the one with Jimmy, it's obvious that parents have a wide variety of opinions about what behaviors they consider healthy and how to encourage that behavior. Some parents would grab the toy back from Jimmy, give him a slap and tell him he was a "bad boy." Others might do nothing but say, "Oh, that's how boys are." Still others might tell Jimmy that it's not OK to grab or push, then model for him a polite way to ask for something he wants.

Some of the main criteria I consider for defining "healthy" are:

- Does the decision protect people's well-being — physically, mentally and socially?
- Does the decision respect the right of others to protect their own well-being — physically, mentally and socially?
- Does the decision take into account the well-being of the community as a whole?

**Showing respect:** The basis for the criteria suggested above is respect: individual self-respect, respect for the right of others to be treated with respect, and respect for the community as a whole — including both children and adults. Respect may be shown in different ways in different cultures, but genuine respect always is freely given and works best if it's mutual.

We can show respect for differences in clothing styles, religious beliefs, customs and abilities. We can be accepting of and learn from these differences, as long as they aren't harming us or the community. If they are harmful, then we need to be working together as a community to create change. The road to peaceful, productive communities begins with us and our children. How do we specifically train our children?

Helping children develop the skills to make healthy choices, as in almost every facet of parenting, demands flexibility. None of the following suggestions for encouraging healthy choices is going to work all the time with all children. Each child's temperament and the circumstances under which a choice is to be made need to be given careful consideration. However, if parents creatively use a variety of such techniques, it's more likely their children will move in positive directions.

**Sharing information:** One of the most important steps is to make sure your children have adequate information. The trick is to do so without preparing long lectures. Children have a remarkable ability to tune out such information.

One of the best ways I've found to share information with children is using what some folks call "teachable moments." When parents see something significant happen on TV or in the neighborhood or hear about something happening at school or among siblings, they take the opportunity to share their own values about the situation and explain to a child what's going on or why things went the way they did. Just a few sentences containing concrete information, a thought-provoking question or a quick word about likely consequences can be very effective.

Even young children can begin to learn what is healthy and unhealthy for their bodies and that each person has the right to be respected. As kids grow older, attention can be drawn to your values around such issues as illegal drug use, sexuality and violence — which unfortunately are so prevalent in the media today.

Make this also an opportunity to let children know where they can go, such as to the library, to find out more information about a particular subject they care about. It's important to let them know that adults seek new information, too. Teaching youngsters the process of locating subjects in the card catalog or computer, in magazines or on microfilm, or how to get information over the phone about some subjects are skills useful throughout life.

Your own life experiences, believe it or not, *can* be communicated to your children, but not always. For example, a decision had to be made about getting a new bed for my daughter Angela. She said she wanted bunk beds. I explained to her that I had experience with bunk beds when I was a child and didn't like them. I had bumped my head on them too often and they were very hard to make. It also was hard to sit up on them to tell stories and they didn't have room for two people to wrestle or snuggle, as she and her sister could do on their double bed.

Angela chose to discount the information and she now has bunk beds. After several bumps on the head within less than a week, she no longer liked her choice. She asked me how I knew that she wouldn't like them — despite the fact that I had already told her. Although Angela did not learn much about bunk beds from me, she did learn something about learning from others' experiences rather than having to make all the same mistakes ourselves.

For my daughter to live with the relatively minor consequences of having chosen bunk beds for the next few years is nothing major. However, the process of sharing with your kids is very important, so they can grow, learn and benefit from your experience and knowledge. I suggested Angela might want to give more consideration to the things that I mention next time she has to make a decision. She said she would and maybe she actually will. Again, we need to remember that learning is a process, not an event.

A third source of information children should be encouraged to tap is the experience of people outside your family. Parents can help create opportunities for kids to talk with other kids their age, or with adults, to share ideas and discuss values. This can be encouraged in a variety of ways at schools, in religious organizations, in scouting. This can also encourage clarification of their own values.

**"What if?" role playing:** One method that works well for encouraging healthy decisions is role playing. You can act out situations with young children in a variety of ways. Sometimes this even works with teens. One category I call "what if" role playing. A parent says something like, "*What if* your best friend wanted you to try a cigarette? Let's pretend I'm Peggy Sue and see how it works out." You and your child can then act out and discuss alternatives and see how the likely consequences feel.

At a group meeting of parents, one mother mentioned that her teen son was invited to go to a party. She didn't feel very comfortable about it because she didn't know a lot of the people who were going to be there. However, some kids from his class were going and she didn't want to tell him that he couldn't go. She said to him, "If you were at a party and there were kids drinking or using drugs, what could you do to keep yourself safe?"

Then she and her son talked about some options. She also used this opportunity to give examples of what "other people" sometimes do to handle difficult situations. "Some young people have an agreement with their parents that if they ever find themselves in what they consider an unhealthy situation, they can call their parents for a ride home using a special key phrase. This won't embarrass them in front of friends, but will tell their parents the importance of getting out of there."

Her son thought this was a great idea and thanked his mom for arranging a special code with him. This technique is good training for on-the-spot decision making in difficult situations and expands the number of options that might be considered by youth.

**"I" messages:** When people disagree, "I" messages can often be used to prevent the disagreement from turning into a serious conflict. "I" messages express how someone feels about a specific behavior and what effect that behavior is having on him or her. For example, I might say to my teenage son who hasn't done assigned dishes on time: "I feel frustrated when the dishes aren't done and it's time to fix dinner. It makes me not want to cook."

Phrasing the statement this way lets him know how I feel and what the consequences might be if the task isn't completed. However, because what I've said doesn't accuse, judge or generalize negative characteristics about him as a person, the door to two-way communication can stay open. He might offer an explanation about why the dishes aren't done or start the task immediately. If not, I've already suggested what might happen.

It might seem a bit awkward to use "I" messages at first, but with practice they can become a common way of structuring conversation to express concerns about a particular behavior. Some factors to keep in mind that help make "I" messages effective are:

- Clearly *own* your own message by using personal pronouns such as "I" and "my."
- Make your messages complete and specific. (Be sure to include any feelings that came before the current feeling — such as frustration preceding anger.
- Make your verbal and nonverbal messages congruent (in tune) with one another.

- Ask for feedback concerning the way your messages are being received.
- Describe the other person's behavior without evaluating or interpreting it.
- Try to avoid using the word "you." Even though a person knows you're talking about something he or she did, impersonal terms tend to create less defensive reactions.

Children can start learning the process of sending "I" messages when they're four or five years old. It's often an effective method for them to use in dealing with disagreements with peers or approaching an adult with a specific concern. For example, a child might say to a friend who has shared a secret she was asked to keep: "I'm disappointed when I share a secret with someone and another person finds out what I said. It makes me not trust sharing secrets anymore."

Two formulas that parents can give children when introducing them to the idea of "I" messages are:

Formula A:

I _____ when _____ .
     (feeling)          (what happened)

It makes me _____ .
               (how it affects you)

Formula B:

It _____ when _____ .
     (feeling)          (what happened)

I feel _____ .
       (description of the action you want)

It's important to remind children that "I" messages don't blame and are honest, open, respectful and understanding. *Not attacking* the other person is necessary for this method to be effective.

Children need to be made aware that using this technique is not a guarantee that two-way communication will happen. Some people are so used to setting up roadblocks that they will respond negatively, no matter how they are approached. However, using "I" messages heightens the probability that a concern will be heard by another person, so everyone should be encouraged to keep using them.

**Natural consequences:** Another way to promote healthy decision making is letting youth experience natural consequences. Dr. Foster Cline and Jim Fay talk about this technique extensively in their book *Parenting with Love and Logic.* Part of their basic philosophy is to pray for children to make mistakes when they're young, so they get practice making choices and having to live with the consequences that are less painful than at an older age.

If the child blows it when given a chance to make an age-appropriate decision, empathy is expressed along with the consequences. This reduces the likelihood that the child will spend time thinking about being angry at the adult, rather than at his or her own decisions.

For example, my showing empathy for Angela every time she bumps her head on her bunk beds isn't difficult, but she has to sleep on them now for at least a couple years. She may not like the consequences, but she understands that it was *her* choice. Similarly, if a child chooses to mistreat a friend, a parent might first try modeling a way to apologize that would make things better. However, if that doesn't work, it's useful to point out in a nonjudgmental way that people often want to leave when others aren't being nice to them.

Some parents tend to "rescue" their children — preventing them from suffering any of the consequences of their own choices. For example, if a child deliberately broke another child's toy, a parent rescuer would replace it, rather than requiring the child to earn money and pay for the damage. If parents don't allow children to feel the impact of their choices, the children won't learn to distinguish between healthy and unhealthy decisions. The basic process of evaluating effectively will be undermined.

It's not always clear for parents exactly what consequences are "natural" for some kinds of mistakes. For example, when a child comes home past supper time from a friend's house, is it a natural consequence for him or her to have to skip supper? Or would it be appropriate not to be able to visit that friend tomorrow?

The flexible parenting challenge here is to be creative in evaluating what would be most effective with each particular child. If a parent is aware a choice is to be made, it's useful to point out the likely consequences in advance. For example, if a child chooses to be slow in getting chores done, the previously agreed upon consequence of not getting an allowance can take effect. This makes it more likely that the child will accept the consequences with less difficulty, even though he or she doesn't like them.

Walking the fine line between talking about consequences and making threats is probably one of the most difficult tasks of parenting. Youth need to understand that when obligations aren't met or effort to meet them is minimal, it causes specific reactions from others. For example, is it a threat or discussion of a consequence to say, "We'll leave for the party when the living room is cleaned up?" The listener's perspective varies, to be sure. But children somehow need to understand clearly that, in general, people can only gain as much *out* of situations as they are willing to put effort *into* them. Life is full of immeasurable exchanges between human beings. All healthy relationships require give and take, both in physical and emotional terms.

Discussing these dynamics specifically and pointing out what you observe in relationships between others can raise youngsters' awareness. With younger children, specifically noting when *they* get to decide something and when *you* get to decide something can foster a "credit, debit" atmosphere. It's fair that we both get some turns making choices in our family. It's critical that parents are honest about situations in which children have no choice — for example, every child is required to be immunized before starting school.

The connection between *how* people behave and *how* others respond is one of the most important aspects of decision making. For youth to grow up believing that others are going to "do" things for them and be "nice," no matter how they behave, would be an injustice to society. Children need guidance in understanding realistic consequences of how they treat others.

When it's difficult for parents to decide what the natural consequences of a decision should be, particularly when it isn't known in advance that a choice will be made, the following guidelines can be kept in mind:

- The closer the consequences are related to the decision that was made, the more likely that a lesson will be learned.

- Demonstrating anger or a judgmental attitude along with allowing natural consequences tends to distract children from understanding the reality that *they* made the choice.
- Intervention is needed to prevent consequences that will do serious mental or bodily harm to youngsters.

**Modeling:** Probably one of the most powerful ways of encouraging healthy decision making among youth is by modeling it ourselves. Explaining simple decisions aloud to children helps them establish a solid framework of their own. For instance, if a parent has mixed feelings on a choice of two activities going on at the same time, the pros and cons of each choice can be shared. Following such examples, children often begin to think out loud as well, increasing opportunities to communicate openly

## ~ *Chapter Seven* ~

# Motivating Youth

**M**ost parents would agree that they want their children to be positively self-motivated, but how can we assist in encouraging this to happen? What makes one child willing to put forth his or her best effort in facing a new challenge while another child is unwilling even to attempt a new task? The answer doesn't come packaged in a form that can be administered to children while they sleep. So, as always, parents are back on that tightrope again, looking for flexible options.

In reality, motivating youth in healthy directions requires a combination of *all* the skills that we have discussed thus far, as well as making sure that children get additional support they need during times of high stress. Keeping this in mind, let's first take a look at what motivates us as adults.

### Our Own Motivation

In devising a plan suitable to support motivational growth in our children, it's useful to think specifically about how we react to things. What makes adults behave in positive ways? Fear of punishment (a speeding ticket or jail term)? Intrinsic rewards (being proud of helping another or doing a job well)? A sense of duty or responsibility (called to a jury, or to war)? The desire to avoid negative reactions from others ("You're *kidding,* Joe!")? Monetary or material rewards ("Time for a bonus, Sue!")? Each of these has probably had a significant effect on your behavior at some point. The same things, in many cases, motivate children.

Examine what you have accomplished in your own life. Have you felt more positively about (a) things you were encouraged to do by others or chose to do yourself, or (b) things you felt forced to do, with the threat of punishment hanging over your head? The first choice is more comfortable for most adults. And children, too.

Stop and think for a moment before speaking to your child. Ask yourself: "How would I react, if someone said to me what I'm about to say, in a similar situation?" If you think your response would be positive, go ahead and speak. If not, you might want to consider alternative ways of dealing with the situation.

## Results Are the Thing

Most parents have loving intentions and do an excellent job of describing how they would like their children to behave in healthy ways. However, the critical factor here is gaining insight into *results.* How is our behavior and the behavior of significant others impacting on our youngsters' motivation? Does a child seem:

- Motivated in healthy directions?
- Motivated in unhealthy or rebellious directions?
- Minimally motivated toward action at all?

**When youth seem motivated in healthy directions:** Thanks are in order when youngsters seem to be learning life skills and are motivated in healthy directions. Studies of the learning process have demonstrated repeatedly that positive reinforcement is remarkably more effective in promoting learning than negative reinforcement. For example, mice learn to run a maze much more quickly if they receive a food reward at the end of the maze than by having small shocks steer them away from wrong turns.

During your child's "good times," it helps to think about what's been happening that might be positively influencing his or her achievements. Try to keep it up.

**When youth seem motivated in unhealthy directions:** Part of balancing on the parenting tightrope is deciding what to do when youth seem consciously motivated in negative directions. This inevitably happens at some point with all children. Examples might include a young child biting someone who has taken a toy away from him or her, two siblings deliberately harassing each other, or a teenager missing supper without notice.

Tempted as we might be to respond to these situations with immediate punishment, it's important to remember that studies also show that when negative reinforcement is used, negative results emerge even if the task is learned.

For example, a rat taught to run a maze by the use of electrical shocks was immediately hostile toward another rat put into the maze — even though the presence of the other had nothing to do with the negative stimulus and their fighting inhibited progress away from the electrical shock.

**When youth seem unmotivated:** Youth who tend to not do much of anything are often not as difficult for parents to deal with as those who rebel or seem motivated in negative directions. However, there should be an awareness that these youngsters might just be very good at suppressing emotions and have such a strong defense system that visible reactions are minimal. Under the surface, there could be a lot of pain from a variety of sources. If this type of behavior continues for a sustained period of time, seek professional evaluation.

## Two-Way Communication

Maintaining two-way communication between parents and children enhances the likelihood of guiding children toward development of healthy motivation.

Some techniques commonly used with the best intentions, but which tend to set up roadblocks and backfire in motivating youth are: making generalizations, ordering youth to do things, criticizing judgmentally, making assumptions and accusing, warning or threatening and not being willing to listen.

These techniques set up a power relationship in which the person using them implies superiority and disrespect, the effect on self-esteem tends to be negative and self-motivation is discouraged in the long run.

For example, accusations are a favorite roadblock with some parents. When a conversation begins by assuming that a child did something wrong, it immediately puts the child (or anyone, for that matter) on the defensive. This often shuts the door to insight into the situation as a whole, invites testing and puts the responsibility for taking corrective action on the accuser. Healthy self-motivation is difficult to develop under these circumstances.

In other cases, a parent might say, "Clean your room right now, Jason!" The responsibility stays primarily with the parent — because if Jason doesn't follow instructions, then it becomes the parent's responsibility to enforce the order. Discussion or negotiations don't present themselves as options in this type of command. And as children get older, they'll tend to build resentment and feel they are not being respected.

As an alternative, a parent might say, "We'll be able to go to the mall as soon as your room is clean." This type of statement lets the child know what needs to be done, encourages promptness through positive reinforcement and leaves the responsibility for doing what's necessary with the child. It is also presented in a way that makes discussion or negotiations at least a possibility. If the child is *not* motivated to clean, consequences are already built in — the parent simply does not take him or her to the mall. Important considerations in this technique are:

- Making sure expectations are developmentally appropriate, breaking seemingly overwhelming tasks into portions.
- Choosing reinforcements that are reasonable, easily attainable and considered desirable by the youngster.
- Being consistent on follow-through (not suggesting something is contingent, when you are going to do it no matter what).
- Refraining from being judgmental when tasks are not done, letting the consequences speak for themselves.
- Indicating positive expectations and respect by the manner in which the child is addressed.

Another healthy alternative is describing the problem objectively, then exploring underlying causes, setting boundaries, and — when possible — discussing solutions that are mutually acceptable as fair.

Becoming self-motivated is a complicated, ongoing process. When children feel they are valued and accepted, two-way communication can flow openly and the sharing of information and guidance promote motivation.

## Expectations

The direction and intensity of the motivation we feel is, of course, influenced by the *expectations* we perceive from those around us. Inappropriate expectations — as in expecting a toddler to sit still for long periods of time — impact negatively.

Similarly, our expectations for older children sometimes grow faster than their development. This encourages youngsters to overreact in a negative way to mistakes. Yet, if children are discouraged from trying new things because they fear reactions to failure or mistakes in the learning process, motivation is damaged. If mistakes or failure at a task are not seen as learning opportunities, progress is slower. Remembering the techniques mentioned in encouraging our children to learn to walk, and recalling our own development, can help us keep perspective on what's appropriate to expect.

Allowing children to struggle a bit, offering assistance, emphasizing progress and expressing confidence that they will be able to achieve with persistent practice establish positive expectations and generally encourage learning. Adjustments need to be made, however, so the conversation comes across in a genuine and age-appropriate way.

The temperament of children varies, as do their moods, so a variety of other techniques might be necessary to promote the development of self-motivation in healthy directions. Some children respond better to being invited to join an activity that you have begun yourself, such as cleaning up after a project. Some youngsters might need a more dramatic approach, such as being asked to come meet the purple dragon in the corner as a technique to make them aware of a dangerous situation. Motivating kids to show consideration of others by asking for their assistance in comforting a child who's been hurt may be appealing to others. One key to not squelching motivation is avoiding making a big issue out of the negative, but focusing on what behavior you do want.

Again, no strategy works all the time, but it motivates children particularly well when you appeal to their desire to exercise some control in a situation. (Sometimes *power* was the real issue to begin with.) Motivating children to actively participate in problem solving can begin when children are three or four. With older youth, parents need to make sure they don't try to *claim* problems that aren't theirs and let teens experience the consequences of their own choices.

One more thing to keep in mind when it comes to motivation is that children often react negatively if adults treat them as if they are younger than they are. For example, there is a tendency for children to resent it and not want to do anything when adults talk to them in "baby talk" or in a singsong voice.

## Motivation and School

Most parents recognize the important influence that education can have on their children's lives, so motivational issues regarding school arise frequently. Although academic and behavioral motivation are intertwined, let's consider them separately.

**Academic motivation:** One of the most difficult tasks parents face before they can promote healthy academic motivation is to accept that the child determines his or her achievement. A parent can offer rewards for test scores or for studying; can threaten or punish for failure to achieve; can support academic efforts by helping with homework, supplying additional materials or paying for tutoring; and can intervene with teachers. But, parents are *not* allowed to turn in homework or take tests, so children themselves ultimately have the control over academic achievement.

Accepting this fact frees parents to consider how they can best promote self-motivation in their children. Some techniques worth trying include:

- Expressing genuine interest in hearing about and seeing school work and celebrating achievement.
- Focusing on what has been achieved positively and asking a child to think specifically about how that learning was done.
- Supplementing "drier" types of learning with a variety of "hands-on" activities that utilize more senses.
- If academic difficulties arise, becoming a parental advocate in analyzing with your children and school staff any physical, mental or social problems that are interfering with learning.
- Modeling a desire to learn and grow academically yourself.
- Sharing reading together on a regular basis. With preschool and elementary children, bedtime stories are great. With older youngsters, newspapers or magazine stories and biographies can reflect how education has affected achievement.
- Help your child develop study habits that are appropriate for his or her age and have realistic goals.

**Behavioral motivation:** Sometimes parents fail to recognize how important social dynamics are as a part of the learning process. Behavior that isolates students from others or is disruptive to the group can damage the learning process for the individual student, both academically and socially, and for classes as a whole. If a child seems motivated to interact negatively or minimally with others, medical issues must be addressed first. After a clean bill of physical health, specific skills can be taught that prepare youngsters to feel comfortable interacting with others, encourage self-management, optimize openness to academic learning and prepare him or her for adult participation in the community.

Healthy modeling by parents or other adults who spend a lot of time with children is probably the most significant way children learn social behavior. Programs at schools and community service organizations can promote skills such as being assertive and negotiating, thus motivating youth to stand up for themselves.

Parents also need to take some responsibility for encouraging a safe atmosphere in our schools and communities. It's hard for students to concentrate on academics when they're concerned for their own safety.

### Affection and Motivation

There is no scientific proof, but much observable evidence that:

- It takes four hugs a day for a child to survive.
- It takes eight hugs a day for a child to maintain.
- It takes twelve hugs a day for a child to grow.

Generally, children feel more motivated in healthy directions when they feel accepted and loved as human beings. Showing affection is one way of communicating these feelings. Respect should be given to what boundaries are comfortable for each child, as their needs vary greatly. But dosages of caring should be offered daily, even to teenagers. And if your affection is rejected or seemingly ignored, don't take it too personally. Examine whether or not there is something you hadn't been conscious of, which needs to be resolved, or whether it's just time for a new assertion of independence from you. If so, hold back somewhat — but don't stop offering affection. Just like the wind, youth moods change frequently. Not offering affection, even if it's rejected, is sometimes construed as a lack of love.

Our arts reflect the strong motivating force that love can be. Although the focus tends to be on romantic love, rather than parental love, it is more difficult for youth to establish relationships motivated in loving directions with others if they haven't had the security parental love can provide.

## Using a Flexible Approach to Motivation

In concluding this chapter, let's look at one more issue from our flexible parental perspective: sleep. Parents are motivated to seek no other activity so diligently. On the other hand, children sometimes seem equally motivated to resist it themselves and prevent parental indulgence.

Sleep is not something you can really force someone to do using high-pressure tactics. Whatever is causing sleep disturbances may be real or unreal. It may affect a child's ability to get to sleep or stay asleep through the night. Regardless, parents need to view the problem with the *intent to learn.*

Medical issues should be ruled out first. Does the child have an ear infection, fever or stomach ache that is making it difficult to sleep? Before a child can talk, it is sometimes difficult to know if something hurts. However, checking temperature and thinking about any changes in behavior or routine — such as pulling on an ear or not wanting to eat — can alert parents to medical difficulties. Older children can, of course, just be asked if they're feeling all right. (If this is done at least a half-hour before bedtime, there's less likelihood that illness will become a technique for manipulation.)

If your child is old enough to talk, discuss whether there's something out of the ordinary bothering him or her. You can't know unless you ask. Sometimes fear or an upsetting experience might be interfering with his or her ability to relax.

For example, a young boy once told his friend that if he opened his mouth while he slept, he would die. Every time this young friend started to fall asleep, his mouth would begin to open and he'd wake up.

This fear was not based on adult reality, but to children such fears can be extremely real. Worries about monsters in the closet or snakes under the bed need to be dealt with in a respectful way. Some simple ways worth trying to calm this kind of fear are:

- Doing checks for the *lurking* evil.
- Using magic spells, stuffed animal guards, rules monsters are required to follow, or other imaginative protective techniques.
- Night lights.
- Assurance that you are close by and would come immediately if there is any trouble.
- Reminding children of their own safe past experiences in bed.
- Letting them know that parents' love protects sleeping children.

Other fears have more basis in reality — an actual frightening experience or one that seemed real in a movie or on TV. Taking some appropriate actions directly can help children regain a sense of control and feel safer. For example, my daughter Angela went to a fire department demonstration about safety and how to get out of a burning house. She was scared to go to sleep because she thought the house might catch on fire. A combination of strategies that work included:

- Reminding her we'd lived five years in this same house with no fires and everyone knew not to smoke or play with matches.
- Reviewing our fire safety rules — making sure she could open the window, climb out on the porch roof and get to a neighbor to call 911.
- Assuring her that our rooms were only three feet apart and if there was a problem, I would come immediately.
- Putting a smoke alarm in her room.

Repetition sometimes makes strategies more effective. Discussion of fears and methods of controlling similar future situations can help relieve stress.

Sometimes parents find no specific incident or fear that causing a child to have problems sleeping. Motivating forces behind the behavior might be:

- Not wanting to miss out on any activities.
- Being too wound up or stressed to relax.
- Testing parental limits.
- Having gotten used to habits that are no longer necessary or desirable.

For example, I nursed my children in the middle of the night — a pattern of getting fed and snuggled at 3:00 A.M. was well established. When they had been weaned and were eating solid food, they continued to wake up in the middle of the night — every night. Similar patterns can easily develop if a child is sick and gets special midnight attention for a while.

Changing a routine rarely happens without a struggle. Hearing children cry is likely to be a part of this process. Parents need to be determined if a new pattern is to be established.

Age, of course, affects what strategies to try. When Angela was not old enough to talk well, the method I found effective in less than a week was lying her down firmly, calmly telling her it was time to sleep, then leaving the room. She would cry. I repeated the same thing every ten minutes until she went to sleep. After several nights of this routine, she began sleeping through the night. With a child this young, some things to be sure have been taken care of before going to bed or during the first midnight scream are:

- Check for binding or uncomfortable clothes.
- Is it likely the baby is hungry, thirsty, needs a diaper change or is too hot or cold?
- Does the child have some object that provides security — a stuffed animal, blanket?
- Has the baby had adequate attention during the day — rocking, snuggling?

Parents have many more options when dealing with older children. It's useful to make a distinction between time with children and time for adults to be alone. A child can understand that it's time for him or her to be quiet and by themselves in their bed or room. Almost everyone wakes up at night sometimes and we need to learn to get ourselves back to sleep on our own. The problem-solving method can be used after making it clear what your values and expectations are: "When parents don't get enough sleep, they start acting like Oscar the Grouch. It also doesn't feel good to get angry with children before they go to sleep. What can we do to make it easier for you to go to sleep and not wake up until morning?" In brainstorming solutions, some of the following might be suggested:

- Mutually agree on a routine — after getting ready for bed, we'll read one story, have two swallows of water, sing one song and have a hug.
- Use stickers to chart desired behavior or other rewards to reinforce movement in a positive direction.
- Set up specific goals and rewards — when you sleep through one night, we'll go to the park; when you sleep through two nights, we'll go out to dinner; and when you sleep through four days in a row, we'll go to the zoo.
- If settling down is the problem, explain that the consequence for not going to sleep by a particular time will move the "getting ready for bed" time up five minutes at a time.
- Use "I" messages to let the children know what effect their behavior is having on you.
- Emphasize that going to bed without a hassle and sleeping through the night are things that "big" kids are able to do. (Don't slide into making children feel *judged* or *put down.*)
- Use an idea your child comes up with all by himself or herself about what will make it easier to sleep.

Some additional prevention strategies for parents to be conscious of are:

- Don't let children take naps too long or too late in the afternoon — kids won't be tired at bedtime.
- Make sure children are getting adequate physical outlets for their energy.
- Have going to the bathroom just before sleeping as part of the routine.
- Make activities done within an hour before bedtime be calming — baths, board games, cards, stories, songs — no running, tickling or wrestling.

Once a positive routine is established, parents need to try to maintain it as consistently as possible. The reward is when kids are truly motivated to make bedtime a close and warm experience.

*~ The Parenting Tightrope ~*

# ~ *Part Two* ~

# Children in Crisis and Under Stress

A car slams on its brakes unexpectedly on the expressway in front of you. Your van swerves, spins around and hits the median. You come to rest facing oncoming traffic. People who saw the accident stop and direct traffic around you until you get off the road. You and your children were all buckled in and everyone is safe, but shaken.

Situations that put this kind of emotional stress on children are almost inevitable. If it isn't a car accident, it's seeing another person seriously hurt, losing a relative or a pet, hearing a frightening argument, or breaking that special toy.

An important part of being a parent is learning how to assist our children in these crisis situations. The Chinese character for crisis contains both *danger* and *opportunity*. Parental reactions can affect both the emotional and physical strength and health of children.

Under some circumstances, children face emotional stress over a sustained period of time — such as with divorce, substance abuse, domestic violence. The intensity of stress varies over time, but specific events periodically create major crisis. Any crisis is a significant emotional event and has the potential of causing ongoing problems if adequate support is *not* available.

After examining crisis more closely in Chapter Eight, Chapters Nine through Twelve will deal with specific situations that invariably cause crisis. Chapters Thirteen through Eighteen will discuss issues that may create an atmosphere of tension, but don't necessarily cause crisis. Following an overview of each topic, the focus will be on parental strategies for minimizing the stress on children. Parents need to recognize that high emotional stress is often closely connected to low self-esteem and troublesome behavior in children.

# ~ *Chapter Eight* ~

# Crisis

**H**ow can parents know when a child is in crisis? An incident that causes crisis for one child might not affect another as seriously.

A practical definition of crisis is any situation that "keeps people from acting as they normally do." Some typical physical symptoms of crisis include changing eating or sleeping habits, shaking, diarrhea, headaches, chills and profuse sweating. Emotional reactions often include an increased level of sensitivity, crying, anxiety, fear, guilt, feeling lost or abandoned, wanting to hide, anger and numbness. Thinking or problem solving may be much more difficult during this time. Children dealing with high stress situations over extended periods may exhibit similar symptoms, as well as have a tendency to be more susceptible to illness. Negative or aggressive behavior are also common.

One of the first steps you can take as a parent after a crisis occurs is to let your children know you are there for them by respectfully acknowledging their feelings. Sometimes adults do not appreciate the full impact various situations have on children and are tempted to deny or minimize seriousness. Telling children "it could have been worse" or "it's not really that bad" only encourages them to hide their emotions, shutting you out and blocking the healing process. It is especially important after a crisis to be more sensitive to learning why inappropriate behavior might be happening, as opposed to just dealing with unusual behavior on a surface level.

Using tentifiers such as "it seems like ..." or "sometimes people feel ... when ..." or "It's possible that ..." allows our children to verify that what we've said is what they're really feeling — or to explain to us that they're feeling another way without contradicting us.

This is also a time to show supportive affection, if your child is willing to accept it. Don't be surprised or feel rejected if your child pushes you away at first. A need to be alone or to be angry commonly accompanies crisis situations. Let your child's reaction be your guide to what he or she needs. Support that might initially be rejected might be acceptable after a while, so don't hesitate to offer a hug again a short time later.

If a parent is in crisis at the same time as a child, it may be a good time to enlist the support of another relative or friend to provide additional care for your son or daughter. It's also important to remember that even if a crisis situation seems to affect only a parent, it inevitably will have *some* effect on children.

The most important tool in helping your child deal with crisis in a healthy way is talking. After the initial shock of the crisis situation has subsided a bit, it is time to approach discussing what happened. Talking about exactly what occurred brings out a sharing of feelings and promotes a healthier perspective. Children often will say they don't want to talk about a crisis situation, but then continue to bring it up. Asking gentle questions about what they felt or asking them to explain the details again can make a great difference in the healing process. Be aware of nonverbal clues youngsters give, as well as what they say, while offering your support. Do not pressure your child to talk about the incident if he or she is unwilling. Additional stress is definitely not needed.

Depending on the impact of the crisis situation, it might take anywhere from a few days to months to return to normal behavior. It's important to see that physical needs such as regular meals and sleep are being met. People in crisis sometimes forget these basic needs. Encouraging a return to participating in somewhat normal activities fairly quickly is useful — not so with pretending the situation didn't happen or not talking about it.

Taking some action when appropriate can also sometimes help. For instance, having your own memorial service for a person or even a pet, and talking about what that person or pet would want for you in the future can help. After an accident, making a list of prevention strategies can help children regain some sense of control and not feel so vulnerable.

No one stays in active crisis for more than about six weeks. If symptoms last longer than this, professional help should be sought before there is a mental or physical breakdown. Time can heal and when it's accompanied by active support, a return to a normal emotional state can happen more quickly. Under circumstances in which elevated stress levels are sustained over an extended period of time, people frequently develop a variety of defense mechanisms, often including denial or isolation, to protect themselves from feeling they are constantly in active crisis.

Some crisis situations arise around serious problems for which there may be a variety of solutions. When people get into crisis, they tend to have tunnel vision. They view situations as having only one way out, or none. This becomes another opportunity for you to share problem-solving skills with your child. After having thoroughly discussed what happened to cause the problem, help your child learn to brainstorm possible solutions without judging them. Have your child think about how he or she handled other crisis situations in the past or how he or she saw others do so. Using impersonal language to broaden possible solutions is often very helpful. For example a parent might say, "When ... happens, some people ..." Then move into letting your child evaluate what would happen if each solution was picked. Your child can then decide which solution seems best and try it. If results are good, congratulations are in order. If not, encourage trying another choice.

This process of working through crisis situations provides children with tools that will be useful to them their entire lives. Libraries often have books on specific crisis situations that can serve as a good example of how to recuperate. Most areas have crisis intervention centers. Don't hesitate to call if you're experiencing crisis yourself or need support in assisting your child through a difficult situation.

# ~ *Chapter Nine* ~

# Grief

When my husband's mother died, my sixteen-year-old stepdaughter felt the pain more than the other grandchildren. As a young child she had spent a lot of time visiting her grandmother by herself. After her grandmother's stroke, my stepdaughter was the one who went to visit her most often and would comb grandmother's hair and talk to the nurses about her care. She wrote a poem for her grandmother and read it amazingly well through her tears at the funeral.

Helping youngsters grieve the loss of a loved one is a difficult task for any parent. Both the age of the child and the closeness he or she felt to the person who died influence the depth of the reaction. Meanwhile, parents can feel overwhelmed balancing family obligations, their own grief and details of funeral arrangements — let alone the confusion, fear and sadness usually felt by youngsters.

So how can parents help their families get through a crisis of grief? Besides the crisis guidelines mentioned earlier (acknowledging youngsters' feelings, talking things out and getting extra support), it's important to remember that grieving is a process.

One of the most common immediate reactions after a death is denial of either the death itself or any outward signs of emotion. This kind of numbness frequently lasts as long as eight weeks after a death.

Facing death's reality, feeling death's pain and beginning to put life back together again is a process that might happen fairly quickly or might continue over the first year after the loss. Building new relationships and becoming more comfortable with the changed situation gradually happen next.

Being able to continue life with a positive attitude and once again feel comfortable are signals that someone has successfully worked through the grieving process.

Children's response to death will, of course, vary according to their stage of development. Although reactions are sometimes similar for children and adults, some special issues in dealing with youngsters to be particularly aware of are:

- Young people sometimes want to avoid dealing with grief at all, continuing life as if nothing has changed.
- Young children are more likely to deny the finality of death.
- Youngsters sometimes feel uncertain about what is expected of them. Is there a "right" or "wrong" way to grieve?
- When exposed to death, young people may get as overwhelmed by the fear of their own death as much as by the loss.

Parents should be familiar with the following typical signs of grief:

- Shock and denial.
- Guilt.
- Anger.
- Loneliness.
- Depression.

- Emotional sensitivity.
- Physical reactions to stress, such as headaches.

If these or other crisis symptoms seem to last for more than about eight weeks, parents should consider seeking additional help. Children may have gotten "stuck" somewhere in the grieving process, and are unable to move in healing directions.

**Strategies to Promote Healing**

Some useful tips for both grieving parents and grieving children are:

- Express feelings and emotions out loud.
- Ask for help
- Accept help.
- Join a support group.
- Be kind to yourself.
- Get plenty of rest.
- Be alert to physical and emotional problems; see a doctor, if necessary.
- Eat healthy foods.
- Set short, then long-term goals for yourself.
- Try new activities.

Death tends to be handled awkwardly in our society. Even adults frequently don't know what to say to someone grieving a loss. To not express any feelings about a loss is common almost immediately after a death. This is unfortunate, because openly talking about feelings and getting the support of others is one of the best ways to promote the healing, growth, renewal and hope.

Books and videos from libraries, health departments or bookstores are available to help children discuss how they felt when the death occurred, how they feel now and what they miss most about the person who died.

Recalling with youngsters a list of things they liked about the person who died, making a picture album or writing a letter to him or her can be an outlet for feelings that have been bottled up. In making suggestions to do these types of activities, it should be made clear to the child that things can be done alone, with one parent or as a family.

Some of the issues that may come up for discussion are:

- What children can't do, now that the person is gone.
- What the child wishes he or she had said or not said.
- What the child wishes the person who had died had said or not said.
- What is missed most.
- What he or she would like to ask the person who died.
- What the child wishes he or she had done or not done.

For some people, keeping a diary about their thoughts after losing someone helps them better understand their feelings and become more comfortable again. A verbal diary with a younger child can provide a similar outlet.

Most importantly, parents need to remember that they can't take care of their children as well if they don't take care of themselves. When available, support from family, friends, clergy and co-workers can be invaluable during the grieving process. Additionally, community crisis hot lines usually can offer referrals. Many communities have support groups at hospitals, health departments or through human service agencies for adults and children. Don't hesitate to make your needs known and ask for assistance in getting through the grieving process. With sufficient support, many can turn a loss into an experience of growth.

## ~ *Chapter Ten* ~

# Suicide

I t's hard to imagine a thought more frightening to parents than having their own child commit suicide. Suicide, however, is the second leading cause of death among teens today (accidents are first). It is estimated that more than one thousand American children and adolescents attempt suicide every twenty-four hours.

Many of the factors contributing to young people feeling so unhappy and hopeless — even that life is not worthwhile — already have been mentioned. But sometimes it's easy for parents to misjudge how seriously certain incidents can affect youngsters. Tunnel vision can prevent youth from seeing that a particularly devastating situation is temporary, or that support is available from others.

Most teens will come into contact with someone who attempts suicide, seriously considers it, or actually succeeds. Most of those who attempt suicide give some clues or talk about it beforehand to friends, teachers or counselors. If parents and their children become familiar with the signs that often precede suicide attempts, the chances of successful intervention improve. Most of those who are suicidal will not try it if they are taken seriously and given help.

The discussion of suicide here is heavily indebted to information contained in a book titled *Preventing Teenage Suicide* by William Steele, MA, (Ann Arbor Publishers, 1983).

One of the most important things to understand when talking about suicide is that *no one can make another person commit suicide.* It also shouldn't be considered another person's responsibility to "save" someone else. Suicide is a **choice** that each individual can only make for himself or herself. Sometimes people are afraid to ask another if he or she is thinking about suicide because they think it will make an attempt more likely. This is a myth. Talking about whether a person is considering suicide and helping connect that person to support resources can often prevent an attempt.

### How Likely is Suicide?

Most youth at some point in their lives will make a statement that suggests suicide in some way. Because the implications of such suggestions are potentially so serious, parents need to be able to acknowledge clues without panicking unnecessarily. The following *risk criteria* apply to everyone but can be particularly useful in deciding what to do about youth.

**The suicide plan:** The more specific a person is about the way he or she will die, the higher the likelihood an attempt will be made.

**The availability of method:** Whenever the method is readily available, the risk becomes higher. For example, a person who says he or she has thought of carbon monoxide poisoning but does not have a car is less at risk than a person who has a car available.

**Location:** The same principle applies. If someone has determined the place and it is accessible, the risk is very high, especially if the location is inaccessible to others.

**Time:** Again, being specific increases risk. Teens most often attempt suicide in their own homes between midafternoon and midnight.

**Ingestion of alcohol or other drugs:** Whenever anyone is drinking or taking other drugs and talking suicide, the risk is very high. Alcohol and other drugs reduce self-control, making the person more impulsive

**Accessibility for rescue:** If a person plans to attempt suicide at a time or place where no one is expected or able to reach, the risk is higher.

**Lack of support:** If the person has no friends or parents who are less than concerned, or if the person refuses to give the information necessary to reach friends or those who could help, the risk is high.

**Loss:** Risk also is high whenever there has been a recent loss and the person is talking suicide. A loss that may not seem significant to us can be very painful for another person, especially when a series of losses have preceded it. Loss may concern a loved one, a friendship, money, a job, a promotion, social status or a pet. For youth, not getting an "A," not making the team, not being accepted into peer groups, or being rejected from a peer group can be significant losses.

**Previous attempts:** Those who have attempted suicide in the past are always high risk.

**Illness:** When chronic physical illness is present, such as diabetes or long-standing emotional problems, the person considering suicide is more at risk.

Potential victims give three basic types of clues when they are considering suicide:

**Behavioral clues:** How they act.
- Sudden changes in behavior.
- Drinking or taking other drugs.
- Decline in school performance.
- Inability to concentrate.
- Withdrawing from others.
- Studying all the time to the exclusion of outside activities and friends.
- Fighting physically with family members.
- Running away.
- Giving away possessions.

**Verbal clues:** What they say.

**Direct:**
- "I feel like killing myself!"
- "Sometimes she makes me so mad, I feel like hanging (shooting, and so forth) myself."

**Indirect:**
- "Everyone would be better off without me."
- "If this happens again ..."
- "I just can't take anymore ..."
- Any denial that problems exist when problems are obvious to others.

**Situational clues:** What has happened.
- Loss of relationship.
- Loss of status (not making grades, or team, or exclusion from peer group).

- Divorce of parents.
- Violence within the family.
- Parent overemphasis on achievement.
- First year of college.
- Period of time immediately following a long bout of depression or hard times.
- Physical problems along with changes in behavior or performance.

## What Parents Can Do and Say:

**Direct approach:** Ask if the person has been considering suicide. If he or she says "no," such an answer can be followed by pointing out some of the things that you have seen that worry you.

If you feel someone might try suicide, even if he or she says it's not true, notify a responsible adult who will listen. Get further assessment or professional help. School counseling offices, religious organizations or human service agencies can usually offer assistance.

**Indirect approach:** Another way of talking to someone considering suicide is to let him or her know that you've thought lately that he or she seems to be "burned out" or bothered by something. If the person you're worried about agrees, you might say something like, "Sometimes people wonder whether all the hard work is worth it." As talk continues, he or she may tell you if they're thinking about suicide.

**Remember:** It's not enough simply to ask questions. You need to convey to that person that there is hope and help available. Be a good listener and show you care. Assist the child in focusing on positive things he or she has done and understanding how important he or she is to you as a son or daughter (relative, friend). Remember, some suicidal people hide their feelings very well. If you feel a person is really not talking about what the problem is or might try suicide, get help. Assistance can come from a suicide or crisis center (call the telephone operator to get numbers), or community mental health agency.

First encourage the person to get help on his or her own or with your support. If they don't agree, get professional assistance anyway.

**Some don'ts:**
- Don't try to make the situation seem OK by telling the person he or she has it better than others.
- Never tell a person that what is being felt is crazy or silly.
- Giving reasons why it is important for a teen or child to live is useful, but don't argue.
- Don't tell a person that to think about suicide is "bad." To tell a person suicide is immoral only serves to make him or her feel more worthless than he or she already feels.
- Don't tell someone that he or she cannot possibly feel as bad as he or she thinks. Adults often assume young people can't feel things in a very strong way. This is not true.
- Don't leave the person alone if you feel there is immediate danger. An agreement not to attempt suicide until some action or help can be gotten is sometimes useful.
- Don't feel responsible for "saving" the person.

Because the negative impact of suicide on both the family and the community tends to be so strong, it's important to share the kind of information presented here as widely as possible.

In the school programs I work in, students are told to "share a secret, save a friend!" This thought is useful for each of us to remember. Life inevitably has pitfalls, but there is potential for each individual to lead a worthwhile life. Supporting others during difficult times is a role each of us can play at some point.

*~ The Parenting Tightrope ~*

# Chapter Eleven

# Domestic Violence

C ruelty sells. Violence is regularly promoted in movies, TV and even through toys and games. However, let's take a closer look at the point when "hurt" sometimes causes serious or permanent damage to children.

- A boy tells a trusted school social worker that his father got drunk and laughed with his friends as he encouraged the family dog to urinate on the boy's leg.
- A girl comes to school with bruises on her arms after her mother shook her during an argument.
- A child regularly comes to school hungry because she is not fed at home.

One of the worst crises a child can face is continual fear of being abused or neglected. Some children face this crisis every day. In Michigan, for example, more than fifteen thousand substantiated cases of abuse or neglect are reported each year. Few such situations are front-page news, but every one of them can have a devastating effect on the children involved. More societal pressure is needed that emphasizes prevention and early intervention.

All parents, school personnel and community leaders must be drawn into this issue. The behavioral problems of children caught in this type of situation can result in major problems for the whole community. It's not mere chance that many prison inmates were abused as youngsters. Laws set limits that are often not fully understood by the community and, in many cases, are not enforced. Because the implications of the damage are so serious, parents need to take a more active role in ensuring the health and safety of all the children in our communities.

The prevailing attitude is that people should mind their own business — that parents have a right to decide how to treat their own children. There are laws, however, limiting the right of people to harm one another. And if all of us have a clearer understanding of some of the dynamics of child abuse, more sensitivity and support will be offered to both children and parents.

Some communities have done a better job than others in educating citizens, law enforcement personnel and social agencies about the specifics of child abuse laws. Further strengthening both our formal and informal systems of dealing with child abuse is essential.

### Thinking about Reasonable

Rarely does anyone grow up in a family in which a parent hasn't lost his or her temper, raised a voice or said something to make a child feel hurt. However, parents have the responsibility of making sure these "hurts" fall within humane and legal limits.

It's important to remember that many people who hurt other family members actually love them. Parents who go overboard with disciplining their children usually haven't been trained in a variety of parenting techniques. Hurtful ways of teaching right from wrong may be the way they were treated themselves as children. For some parents, it's the only way they know.

In other cases, stress and uncertainty about how to handle difficult situations can result in loss of control. However, permanent damage is done when violence or neglect go unchecked. Help is needed in learning how to make changes or set limits without using harmful methods.

## Understanding Limits

It's useful to categorize in three ways the kinds of hurts that sometimes go beyond reasonable boundaries in families:

**Physical hurt:**
- Very hard spankings.
- Hitting with a belt or brush.
- Slapping.
- Throwing things.
- Kicking.
- Burning.
- Shaking.

**Emotional hurt:**
- Screaming.
- Excessive criticizing.
- Not loving.
- Favoring one family member over another.
- Lack of hugging, affection.
- Disrespecting.

**Neglectful hurt:**
- Not providing enough food.
- Not providing adequate clothing.
- Not providing sufficient medical care.

- Not cleaning younger children regularly.
- Allowing children unreasonable power
  to do as they please.
- Not providing sufficient supervision.
- Making dangerous objects accessible to children.

That's a reasonable list, I think most anyone would agree. Yet a parent in one of my classes openly advocated forcing a child's hand into an open flame to teach him that fire was dangerous. This parent talked about how he had been raised similarly and didn't think there was anything wrong with it. The kind of terror and mistrust such methods can cause in children can be devastating, especially if done often.

Clearly, millions of parents and parents-to-be need education in nonviolent parenting skills. We must teach our own children that:

- Hurting others physically or torturing them
  mentally is not acceptable behavior.
- It's impossible to live with someone and never
  disagree or get mad at them.
- There are ways to vent angry feelings without
  exceeding reasonable limits in terms of hurt.
- People who use violence don't usually change
  without help.
- Assault is a crime, even if it is done to family members.
- Using violence generally makes others
  feel disrespected.

## Action Steps

Parents must be made aware of what they can do if they find themselves in a violent situation, or if they observe others amid violence. A child who sees violence being done to another person can be as damaged as if the violence were being done to him or her. Parents also must share the following approaches with their children for dealing with any violent situation.

*Possible actions by yourself:*

- Leave the situation or try to get to a safe place (behind a locked door, for example) until the situation changes.
- Try to calm the situation by talking.
- Try to protect or defend yourself physically, if no weapon is involved.
- If others might hear, screaming fire can draw attention (again, when no weapon is involved).

*Possible actions supported by family or friends:*

- Call or have some way to signal a friend to ask for help in getting you out of the situation.
- Subdue or restrain the violent person with the help of friends or other family members.
- Escape any way you can and run to a friend or relative's house.
- Get someone the violent person respects to talk to him or her about their behavior when they're not in the heat of anger.
- Move to a friend or relative's house until the person gets some help controlling his or her violence.

*Possible actions supported by community resources:*

- Call the police.
- If the violence is directed toward children or observed by them, call Protective Services after the violence subsides.

- Call a crisis intervention center as soon as possible to discuss the incident and get referrals to community resources.
- Begin getting counseling or therapy for yourself and the abuser — if possible — through community organizations (religious groups, human services agencies, community mental health).
- Join a support group for people in similar situations.

Again, it is extremely important to remember that a pattern of violence seldom stops unless outside help is obtained. In fact, violence tends to escalate from one incident to the next, interrupted by a brief period during which the abuser feels apologetic. An incident might be triggered by anything that makes the abuser feel threatened. For instance, when parents feel a lessened ability to control growing children, they sometimes try harsher punishments. Other times, particularly when substance abuse is involved, almost anything can start trouble. When an adult family member is abused and doesn't seek to change the situation, it encourages the abuser to abuse the children.

Neglect almost must be extreme before community members recognize it. But behavioral problems are almost inevitable if parents spend almost no time with their children and don't make sure that their basic needs for food, clothing and shelter are met. In some cases, a lack of affordable child care causes some parents to neglect their children or expect them to take on too many adult responsibilities at a early age. Parents who work but do not make enough to pay for child care are in an awkward position. Our communities need to push for more recognition of this problem and implement strategies to improve the situation. Parental substance abuse is another common cause of neglect. Children who don't get adequate parental attention for positive behavior are tempted to draw negative attention.

## Community Responsibility

If you see a parent publicly abusing a child, an attempt might be made to empathize with the parent's frustration and to give an example of a technique you used to effectively handle a similar situation with one of your children. Before doing this, consider your own safety and approach the person respectfully.

Distraction of any sort can frequently interrupt what's going on and encourage the person to think more consciously about what he or she is doing. If you sense something extreme happening in a neighbor's house, an anonymous call to Protective Services or an informal suggestion about a series of parenting classes being offered in the community during a nonvolatile time might be useful.

Again, let me emphasize that the pressure of violence does not mean an absence of love. However, for the health of our communities, we need to do whatever we can to discourage violence against one another.

*~ The Parenting Tightrope ~*

# ~ *Chapter Twelve* ~

# Divorce

W hen Steven was two years old, his parents weren't getting along well. They decided to divorce. At first, Steven stayed with his mother and spent time with his father every other weekend. He loved both of his parents very much. By the time Steven was five, he saw his father only on occasion. Dad wouldn't always show up when he said he was going to. By Steven's ninth birthday, he no longer saw his father.

Such scenarios have become common. One of every four children born today is predicted to spend at least some time living in a single-parent family before the age of eighteen.

Children whose parents divorce have their own tightrope to walk. On the one hand, events beyond their control have broken up the family they have known. On the other hand, children tend to feel that they really had some control over the situation — that the divorce is their fault. If they just hadn't caused trouble, had not argued with their siblings or had given Dad more hugs, the divorce wouldn't have happened.

Unlike crises involving neglect, or substance abuse or a death in the family, divorce usually creates a series of somewhat more minor crises that go on for years after the actual separation. Parents can help children work through feelings of insecurity and guilt by talking with them openly about these issues. When possible, it's useful to arrange for each child affected to talk to an impartial counselor at least a few times.

Besides keeping in mind the crisis strategies mentioned earlier, here are some important specifically in divorce situations:

- Try to minimize hostility between parents, particularly in the presence of children.
- Make it clear that the parents are divorcing one another, not giving up their role as parents.
- Take care of your own mental well-being and see that the health of your children is also being taken care of, even if you can't do it yourself.

Hurt and hostility are almost always felt by parents who divorce. However, once a divorce is set in motion, it's less difficult for children if they don't have to listen to parents' complaints about each other or view open expressions of hostility.

If parents are willing to get counseling together to work out the details of the divorce, rather than relying solely on advice from lawyers, it may make things easier for all concerned. Having an impartial person reflect what each person is saying and represent the interests of children can be invaluable.

Parents don't have to like each other to be courteous, assertive (rather than aggressive) and respectful in getting necessary business handled efficiently. It does not help if children consistently are told negative things about the other parent, even if what is being said is true. If one spouse isn't open to this more neutral type of interaction, the other must appeal to limit hostilities for the protection of the youngsters.

When divorcing parents are able to make it clear that they're not giving up their role as a parent, it tends to make the separation less unsettling for kids. Minimizing children's fear that the loss of their family will be accompanied by the loss of parental love is healthier, even if it doesn't always turn out to be true in the long run.

If children are given input into visiting arrangements, their additional "new home," the division of toys between houses, and so on, it can help them gain some sense of balance and control in their lives more quickly.

One of the most important things for parents to understand in a divorce situation is that as children enter each new developmental phase of life, they have to work through various issues that arose as a result of their changing family.

For example, when a child whose parents divorced when he or she was three reaches puberty, he or she will have to address such issues as:

- Why did my parents get divorced?
- Can I have healthy romantic relationships
  with members of the opposite sex?
- Is there such a thing as a lifetime commitment
  to marriage?

Gaining perspective on such issues becomes even more complicated when a parent starts dating or if one parent is no longer actively parenting. Then the whole question of the loss of love, the child's concept of his or her own value, and what role he or she plays in the family also need to be dealt with at this new developmental stage.

It is sometimes difficult for a parent experiencing his or her own emotional turmoil to be the emotional support for a child. As with any crisis situation, don't hesitate to get assistance from others for yourself or for your children. Most areas have crisis intervention centers operating twenty-four hours a day.

School personnel or county community mental health offices can help or give referrals to local agencies offering support groups or Big Brother/Big Sister programs.

Giving children the opportunity to express themselves with an impartial counselor can help them accept the finality of the divorce. This issue, however, is another that often needs discussion at each new developmental level.

In any counseling situation, it's important that a trusting relationship form between counselor and client. If this doesn't seem to be happening after a few visits, consider changing counselors rather than giving up the idea of counseling.

Oakland County Circuit Court in suburban Detroit developed a program called *SMILE.* Divorcing parents are presented with reasonable guidelines for interaction that are aimed at protecting the well-being of children. The impartial source often makes these suggestions more easily acceptable to parents.

Libraries and bookstores have numerous books discussing divorce written for both adults and children. See this book's bibliography for several titles.

# ~ *Chapter Thirteen* ~

# Stepfamilies

**F**ifty years ago the stages of Broadway were a-tremble with the thrill of romantic love, of seeing that stranger across a crowded room and knowing this was that magic moment. As in "Some Enchanted Evening" from *South Pacific,* notions of romantic love are still very strong in our society — even in the '90s. Our music, our media and our gossip more often than not concentrate on "love." Research has documented that people tend to be healthier in our society when they feel well loved. However, our high divorce rate offers painful proof that "ideal" love isn't all that it takes to sustain a marriage over the years. Actually living with someone, rather than just dating, creates entirely new dynamics. And when two adults enter a relationship coming from situations in which one or both of them have been through a divorce, have had children with another person or grieved the death of a spouse, interactions are complicated immediately.

Each situation is unique, but here are some common feelings that usually arise when a stepfamily or blended family is formed.

## Children's Feelings

- The need to defend their right to their natural parent's love and time.
- Grief over a loss of their family as they knew it.
- Missing the parent that they're not with.
- Blame or guilt.
- Resistance to change.
- Worry that liking a stepparent is equivalent to being disloyal to a biological parent.
- The need to regain some sense of control over their own lives and the space in which they live.

If a parent went through a significant amount of time with no romantic interest in his or her life, a child almost always sees a new partner or siblings as competition for attention from the child's natural parent. Yet, working through such feelings is required to successfully build a step- or blended family.

Most children grieve over the loss of their original family. Youngsters long for an idealized version of their life before the divorce. This issue might not yet be resolved as the new family is forming. In other cases, when one natural parent has died or has completely severed the relationship with his or her children, a certain amount of resentment and insecurity is almost inevitable.

Placing blame is frequently a way children try to regain some sense of control over the changes that are happening in their lives. If something is someone else's "fault," then emotions can have an outlet for expression, even if inappropriately placed. For instance, the separation of biological parents is often blamed on a new partner, even if he or she didn't enter the picture until after a divorce was final.

Guilt is a similar emotion turned inward. It can be a terrible burden if a child feels responsibility for not being "good enough" to keep parents happy or thinks he or she caused the original family disruption by fighting with siblings. Getting caught in either blame or guilt can be very disruptive in trying to form a new family.

The natural human tendency is to resist change. This is exaggerated among children — particularly if change in the past has appeared negative to them.

### Parents' Feelings

- The need for time and energy to nurture the love that has brought this new family together.
- Anxiety about how relationships will work among other family members, both children and adults. Discipline and power are of particular concern.
- The difficulty of establishing realistic expectations when old issues about previous relationships have not been worked through. There is frequently a range of negative emotions that is easily reawakened.
- A yearning for stability. Most people make commitments to a new family in an effort to feel secure in knowing what to expect from life. The need to feel a sense of teamwork with a partner and have active support are ideals usually sought.

Aside from these feelings, some additional factors often affect the atmosphere in any step- or blended family. One of the most important is recognizing that just because two adults have grown to love each other and decided to marry does not mean that the other people involved in their families will love or even like each other. Warm feelings cannot be forced on others. However, they can be encouraged, nurtured and given time to grow.

## Transitional Strategies

It helps to keep in mind that:

- There already was a relationship between at least one of the children and a parent *before* the current adult couple's relationship began.
- Often, more than two parents are involved in the new situation. Civilized interactions with ex-spouses can help minimize negative tensions.
- Step- or blended families have different family histories and — at first — no shared experiences.
- Frequently children must adjust to spending time in two different households, even if only for short visits.
- It is difficult, especially at first, for people to know exactly what roles are expected or acceptable in the new family.

Until stepparents have well-established relationships with their stepchildren, it's usually better for the natural parent to take primary responsibility for disciplinary matters. This helps minimize resentment.

Family meetings can provide the opportunity to solve problems and promote healthy communication in any family, and are particularly useful here.

In starting the family meeting process, the first step is setting a specific schedule when everyone can spend some unhurried time together. If teenagers are involved, even this level of commitment may be challenging.

Establishing ground rules for the meeting is next. Simple guidelines that are important to include might be:

- Only one person talks at a time.
- Everyone gets a chance to share their feelings.
- Each person speaks for himself or herself.
- No put-downs of other family members allowed.
- What is discussed stays within the family, unless it is something a member wants to share about himself or herself.

This last guideline, which really deals with confidentiality, is particularly important. One child, for instance, might bring up the issue of his stepbrother wetting the bed in the room they share. If he later resurrects this conversation in front of his stepbrother and a group of friends it would be very hurtful. Communication would not be comfortable, to say the least.

Meetings can be started merely by saying something like, "Does anyone have anything they would like to share or discuss with the rest of us?"

Especially when you've just started having meetings, a short time might be spent sharing information about such things as expressing feelings, understanding roadblocks to communication or how to send "I" messages that tell how you feel about a specific behavior and how it affects you. When concerns are raised, going through the organized problem-solving method can be very productive.

Some issues in step- or blended family situations that frequently cause concern among children include:

- Feeling blamed too often for things that go wrong.
- Hearing a parent and stepparent fight.
- Feeling that all children are not being treated fairly.
- Having stepsiblings mess up your possessions.
- Having to share a room when stepsiblings visit.
- Having feelings of not being wanted.
- Being told what to do or disciplined by a stepparent.
- Feeling it's up to one particular family member to make the new family succeed.

Dealing with these issues openly in meetings can help a family establish the basis for setting reasonable guidelines appropriate for any situation in which people are going to live together. What is expected of family members in terms of both their treatment of one another and household responsibilities can be included, such as:

- Being courteous and respectful.
- Recognizing each sibling's right to have personal possessions and a commitment to treat shared items with care.
- Allowing every person the right to some privacy.
- A willingness to hold honest and open discussions about disagreements that arise.

Appropriate consequences for breaking the "rules" can also be decided. Some flexibility in consequences may be necessary to accommodate various ages of family members. For example, a loss of a privilege might last longer for a twelve-year-old than it would for a six-year-old.

As with any consequence, the closer it can be tied to being a natural result of what was done, the more effective it usually is in altering behavior. For example, there would be a definite connection between coming home late from a friend's house and a punishment of not being able to go there the next afternoon.

Family meetings tend to work best with school-aged children, but even a three-year-old can participate actively, if given the opportunity to express himself or herself.

Teenagers are particularly sensitive to such issues as power and judgment. Each person needs to feel that his or her concerns will be given serious thoughtful consideration by the group.

Another important way to encourage more positive relationships in a new family is to have both parents spend some individual time with each child. This allows development of shared experiences and time for some positive feedback, uncluttered by everyday hassles such as forgetting to put dirty clothes in the hamper. Carving out this time is sometimes difficult — particularly for working parents — but it is well worth the extra effort.

*~ The Parenting Tightrope ~*

## ~ *Chapter Fourteen* ~

# Effective Discipline

T he biblical shepherd's staff, or rod, was a tool used for stability while the shepherd walked over rough terrain and for guiding the sheep in the right direction. The rounded crook was used to pull sheep away from dangerous situations. I've never seen a shepherd pictured beating his sheep with the staff.

Yet many parents still follow the adage, "Spare the rod, spoil the child." They choose to hit their children with hands, belts, hairbrushes or paddles, rather than offering firm, but gentle guidance. Some of these parents swear that no other corrective measure will work. In fact, when physical punishment has been well established as the chosen method, a switch to another form of discipline will take some time to become effective. It's worthwhile to make the change, particularly when you look beyond your own home at the tide of violence in our nation.

Think about it carefully. Any adults would agree that being physically assaulted is the epitome of disrespect. How many of us would be willing to accept a simple slap across the face or a rap on the back of the head from our supervisor at work? More importantly, would this be the best way to get us to do things better?

Yet, some parents expect children to accept slaps on the hands and face or spanks on the bottom as a normal, "everyday" lesson in doing as they're told.

Too many times I've seen a parent grab a youngster who has hit another child, then proceed to hit the youngster, while yelling that it's wrong to hit. Talk about a confusing message! Relying on physical punishment also loses its impact as children become older. My son was both bigger and taller than me by age thirteen. It would have been very difficult for me to continue to use physical discipline at that point, but it certainly didn't mean that my son no longer needed any disciplining.

The media in this country glorify violence as a problem-solving method on a regular basis. Television cartoons, for instance, have been documented as portraying an average of twenty-eight instances of violence per minute. Monitoring what's watched and limiting exposure time are both important, but there are also some lessons that can be learned if a parent is there to help analyze the violent behavior depicted.

Everyone, including children, wants to feel respected by others. "Respect" includes a recognition of personal value, accompanying rights and acknowledgment that each person is capable of contributing to the well-being of the community. Youth must be taught to realize that to get respect, they must be willing to give it to others.

Do we want to have our children grow up feeling that respect comes from being more powerful or more violent than others? How would this contribute to a society where we live in increasing fear and isolation from one another?

The parental challenge is to teach our youngsters to care about our communities and to protect themselves without encouraging their use of violent behavior on others. Everything in my personal and professional experience suggests that subjecting a child to violence — however well-intentioned — is not the place to start.

## Parental Attitudes

All children are going to test out hurting others at some point. Usually when children are young, they will strike out at someone in frustration or try to use another child as a teething ring. How we respond to such behavior, I believe, has an important impact on helping our children understand the difference between what is socially acceptable and what is not. If parents respond to aggressive behavior by trying to make a joke of it — "Boys will be boys" — and allowing it to continue, the message will be that the behavior is acceptable.

If, on the other hand, the response to hitting, biting or kicking is firm physical restraint and an explanation on how this behavior makes the other person feel, the nonviolent learning process has begun. The message from parents is clear in this case, not confusing as it is when parents model aggression while saying it's wrong. Modeling acceptive alternatives to the behavior is also useful. For instance, with a toddler a parent might say, "It works better when people ask someone to move over nicely, rather than push them."

The word "process" is particularly important here, because it is unlikely that one incident will eliminate the child's experimentation with hurting others. However, I have found that with consistency this method works very well.

Just as all children will test the limits of violence, it's not unusual for parents occasionally to respond to their child's aggression inappropriately. For example, many years ago Amanda, then six years old, and I disagreed about something now forgotten. We both started to raise our voices when she hauled off and hit me. She had never done anything quite like this before and she happened to hit me in a way that sent intense pain through my body. Impulsively, I picked her up, put her over my knee and spanked her. I had seen this happen many times with other children when I was growing up.

Amanda was caught totally off guard. She had only been spanked a few other times in her life, strictly limited to dangerous situations.

After we cried together, we talked about how each of us felt about this incident. Then we both apologized and agreed that we would find other ways to work things out when we disagreed. That was the last spanking I've given and will do all in my power never to respond that way again to a child.

Parents have a responsibility to use patience and self-control themselves and to teach their children to do so, as well. Physical hurt is not necessary to having well-disciplined children.

## Apologizing

The incident with my daughter brings up an issue that I frequently hear raised by parents who tend to use physical punishment on their children: the question of whether it's OK for parents to apologize to their children.

Some people aren't secure with the power they have as a parent. They feel that to admit they've made a mistake or apologize to their children will make them too vulnerable. They fear that their children would see this as a sign of weakness and take advantage, and that apologies would undermine the respect their children have for them.

I've found just the opposite to be true. When children make mistakes, parents usually want them to apologize, to make a commitment not to do whatever it was again and to change their behavior in positive directions. When parents admit they're human, too, and don't beg forgiveness but rather offer to make an effort to do things differently in the future, it usually increases their children's respect. In fact, it models desired behavior.

## Problem Solving and Decision Making

Another way parents can help reduce violence is by helping children learn the healthy problem-solving model discussed previously. For example, when a young child grabs a toy from someone, stop the interaction and explain, "When someone wants a toy from another person, asking for it nicely often works well." Usually this opens the door to either sharing or further negotiations.

With older children, helping them understand the impact their words are having on others can often make for more peaceful interaction. An example of a message that offers insight into a situation without attacking someone would be: "When I hear people putting each other down, it makes me mad. We should all be able to feel good about ourselves without making others feel bad."

Similarly, youth need to be trained in how to respect others while at the same time standing up for their own rights in peaceful ways. For example, parents can do role plays that allow children to practice for the almost inevitable experience of having another child hurt them. "I don't like it when people punch me on the arm that hard, even if they're just playing. It makes me want to stay away from them."

Involving kids in group sports or even board and card games can assist youth in developing good sportsmanship and the self-control to lose "gracefully," without violence.

## The Schools

Some schools are beginning to teach conflict resolution and to set up peer mediation programs. Classroom programs that introduce students specifically to a variety of communication and problem-solving skills are also being introduced in some schools, but not as extensively as they need to be.

Results of these programs have sometimes been dramatic. For example, at one high school fights were becoming a difficult problem among students from a wide variety of cultural and socio-economic backgrounds. Leaders from various groups were chosen to be trained as peer mediators. With the new method of student-centered conflict management in place, physical fights almost completely disappeared. Trained teen mediators spoke openly about how they'd never known how similar their own concerns were to those of students in other groups.

With a younger group of students, a ten-session Peer Relationships program helped alter the atmosphere of intimidation in the classroom. Clear guidelines were established for students' treatment of one another. School changed drastically for one student who had been the favorite scapegoat, as well as for others who feared they might be next.

Time and again we've found that in many instances youngsters who act violently toward others face an unresolved issue that makes them feel uncomfortable — such as divorce, loss of a loved one or an alcoholic in the family. The violence is simply a symptom of the underlying problem that needs attention. School personnel must be encouraged to make contact with parents of troubled students. If counselors approach parents in a concerned rather than a judgmental way, insight may be shared into the child's difficulties. Whether this happens or not, families can at least be made aware of support services available through the school and in the community.

It also is useful for parents to become involved in the schools, offering special skills and support where possible. Parents whose jobs prevent them from participating actively in the classroom during the day can still participate in evening PTA or PTO meetings or special activities, such as a Saturday school cleanup.

### Other Community Institutions and Organizations

Every business or human service agency has a stake in lessening the violence in our communities. Partnerships that keep youngsters involved in constructive activities on a regular basis can go a long way in deterring violence. In some areas, business personnel are going into schools or recreation centers and offering tutoring in such subjects as computers, math and science. Mentoring programs are another way of offering youth extra support.

Politically, the whole community can lobby to encourage development of more programs that allow youth to get some job experience while they are still students. Such programs can benefit both students and businesses and bridge the gap between the worlds of school and work.

Community recreation centers have facilities to offer a wide variety of challenging and constructive activities. Some do a terrific job. Unfortunately, sometimes adequate personnel are not available to run activities. In other cases, personnel are not willing to put in the extra effort it might take to really make a difference in a community. Volunteering to assist at a recreation center or letting personnel know specifically what activities would interest your child is often helpful. Youth involved in interesting, constructive fun are much less likely to be led in negative directions. Changing the mentality in our society isn't going to happen overnight, but the time to begin making that change is now. Parents can be a major motivating force.

## ~ *Chapter Fifteen* ~

# Sibling Rivalry

**W**hy can't you keep your room clean like your sister does?"

What parent hasn't compared one child with another, silently if not aloud? (And, if there aren't any siblings, the neighbor's child will do!)

Differences? They certainly are always present among siblings. Differences in age, temperament, social skills and current developmental stage. So what's the problem with a little friendly competition?

The problem lies in the word "friendly." More often than not, these differences provide fertile ground for growing resentment and hostility, even if parents are careful about what they say. If stepbrothers or stepsisters are involved, it can be even worse. The long-term tension caused by unhealthy management of sibling rivalry frequently leads to periodic crises and undermines positive self-concepts.

So what might parents keep in mind or do to discourage sibling rivalry and promote supportive relationships among their kids? A good first step is to consider what your child's perspective might be.

## Family Expansion

How does it feel when a new sibling is brought into a family? I heard a very effective analogy to help adults understand how a sibling's birth emotionally affects an older brother or sister. Adults at a workshop were asked to picture their spouse bringing home another husband or wife to live with them. Imagine the reactions you would have, even if it were explained to you that this person would help with responsibilities and that you would still be loved "just as much." Imagine further that following this wonderful introduction, the new member of your household then proceeded to demand most of your spouse's attention. A good trooper might eventually adjust, but the period of adjustment would be a killer.

It is natural for any child to feel the birth of a sibling is an invasion of their lives. Recognizing their feelings and letting them know you understand that getting used to a new family member isn't easy will help. Whenever possible, carving out special time for older children on a regular basis can also assist in the transition.

The family position into which children are born sometimes affects how they interact with siblings. First children often get more undivided attention and the impression that they are truly valued more easily than those who follow. A child whose birth is followed quickly by another or who ends up as a middle child while still in infancy or the young toddler stage almost inevitably gets less attention than a child who is three or more years old before the birth of a younger sibling.

The child's response may be to push for attention, or a reversion to "baby behavior" or outright hostility. It's useful for parents to respond in a way that recognizes their child's feelings but lets him or her know clear behavioral limits, gradually guiding him or her toward developing a positive relationship with a sibling. Enabling the older child to "help" with the baby and reinforcing "big kid" behavior can go a long way.

Conversation such as: "It's sure terrific that you know how to put on your own coat already," or, "Would you like to give the baby her bottle while I hold her?" can help ensure a child that he or she hasn't lost value in the family. However, parents accepting "no" to helping in a nonjudgmental way is important, too. Giving children a real choice about their contribution can arm them with some sense of control. People in our society are healthier when they feel respected and voluntarily support the members of a group.

## Parental Strategies

The basic foundations for healthy families — such as respect and allowing children the opportunity to express themselves and gradually assume responsibilities — apply in any household situation. But certain aspects of childrearing are particularly important when it comes to dealing with siblings.

**Avoiding comparisons:** First and foremost, parents should try not to compare kids with one another. Recognizing each child's individuality and speaking to that specifically is more effective in molding behavior.

If comments on specific behavior can be given when kids are by themselves, it often works better. For instance, when my older daughter did a particularly good job helping with some younger children, sharing my appreciation when her siblings weren't around made it more special. Many times siblings will interpret omission of a comment about them as criticism or not caring as much for them. For example, if one sibling hears a remark to another about what a good job was done on cleaning a room, it's almost automatic for him or her to assume failure at a similar task because nothing was said. Along the same lines, corrections can seem harsher or surely more embarrassing if done around others.

**Avoiding overdoing it:** A second important consideration is not "overpraising" or "overcriticizing" behavior. No child is "always" perfect or "always" a troublemaker. If "excellent" and "awful" are overused it discourages youth from developing a more internalized sense of pride and motivation. It also encourages competition for attention — either positive or negative. The defensiveness or frustration among siblings if either of these behaviors becomes a habit upsets the balance that all kids need to feel between successes and mistakes. Parental honesty becomes questionable under these circumstances, too.

**Avoiding kid classification:** Categorizing our children and making assumptions that this one is "clumsy and breaks things" or that one is the "artist in the family" can cause unnecessary tension among siblings and keep them from developing into being their best. For example, if a child believes parents view a sibling as "doing everything right all the time," he or she may feel there's no point in trying. Others might react by competing but never really developing the healthy self-confidence that goes along with feeling accepted and valued as an individual.

It's also important for parents to be aware of sibling dynamics when dealing with "gender issues." For instance, some parents don't think it's OK for boys to play with dolls. If we want fathers to participate actively in parenting their children, don't boys need the opportunity to experiment with that role? Girls in elementary school often do well in math and science, but the numbers interested in these areas dwindle in high school. Are we inadvertently discouraging girls from contributing to society in these important fields?

I had learned by late elementary school that boys didn't like girls to beat them at games, so that if you wanted to be popular, you let them win at least part of the time. I also noticed that by sixth grade many girls had begun to define their own worth in terms of how they were valued by boys rather than by what their own skills or talents were. Boys who weren't good at sports were often called "sissies."

When my daughter was three she was a Ninja Turtles fan and wanted to be a turtle for Halloween. Then she started preschool. Within a short time, she had learned that "playing Ninjas" was a boys' game, so she quickly lost interest. I don't particularly like the violence associated with the turtles, so her losing interest didn't bother me. But how much other potential is being lost through this same process of gender stereotyping at home or in school.

Healthier relationships among siblings are encouraged when there is equal opportunity for each child to develop along lines that interest them. Should girls automatically miss out on sharing certain special activities with their Dads, or boys with their Moms, just because of gender? By being more conscious of how we behave, we can at least help our kids be aware of these dynamics so they can make informed choices.

**Heading off squabbles:** By living in the same house siblings often spend a great deal of time together. It's inevitable that they will disagree or want the same toy at the same time. How can parents minimize negative interaction?

Modeling and encouraging use of the problem-solving methods discussed earlier are particularly useful with siblings. Again, brainstorming on what kinds of behavior are acceptable and making sure that reasonable limits are agreed upon are a necessity.

If various methods of negotiations have been thoroughly explored, by the time youngsters are five or older you should probably try to let siblings work things out themselves whenever possible. It's particularly important that siblings go for "win-win" results or solutions in which no one feels that they have lost out completely. At first you might want to ask for a report on the results to ensure that no one is being treated unfairly. Occasionally, I find it useful to suggest that I'll be happy to dictate my own solution for the problem if the kids can't work it out. Predictably, I rarely get that chance.

**Handling jealousy:** "It's not fair! I have to do more chores than her!" If it's not about chores, it's about a present one child got or an activity that only one can do. Possibly every sibling ever born has complained about being treated unfairly at some point.

Acknowledging feelings, offering clear explanations about decisions and being open to suggestions regarding how things might be changed in the future if they truly are inequitable can help minimize jealousy. Children also need to be reminded that what's fair is not always a case of treating each sibling "the same." A ten-year-old is just much more capable than a four-year-old of doing certain chores. A chocolate candy bar that's a real treat to one child, might make another sick. A privilege that's reasonable for an eleven-year-old might be unsafe for an eight-year-old.

Discussing with children that parents do not always have control over what gifts or opportunities are offered to siblings from outside the family is important, too. Involving children in brainstorming ways they can turn "lemon" situations into "lemonade" is good practice for adult life. None of us always gets what we want, when we want it. For instance, a child who watches a sibling walk out the door to a birthday party can be encouraged to take good advantage of the special time alone with a parent to do a special craft project or take a trip to the park.

**Creating special opportunities:** One of the most important things parents can do to promote healthy relationships among their children is to make sure all siblings have chances to share in doing fun things together. Reading stories, playing family games, swimming, making things, singing or going on special outings together all are ways of creating memories or traditions that encourage healthy emotional bonding.

In today's society, families are often busy with work, school and other responsibilities. It takes conscious effort to focus on spending time together as a family. Watching television often fills up all spare time in which family members could be interacting. There sometimes is resistance to flicking the off button, but my family has found that many worthwhile activities happen just by limiting TV time.

*~ The Parenting Tightrope ~*

## ~ *Chapter Sixteen* ~

# Children with Special Needs

A ll children at some time in their lives will face a specific medical crises. Something — a broken leg, perhaps — is likely to impose physical restrictions. Now consider the cases of Allen, Ben and Janice:

- Allen was born with arms that stopped at the first joint and with three-digit hands.
- Ben's mother used crack cocaine throughout her pregnancy. After seventeen months of foster care, Ben was still learning not to bang his head against his crib
- After failing to learn how to read during first and second grade, Janice, with an IQ over 130, was diagnosed as dyslexic.

These three youngsters are examples of children who face ongoing limitations that require special care from parents, care they need to achieve as healthy and happy a life as possible.

Rather than specifically dealing with various difficulties such children face, this chapter will briefly highlight a few useful points for consideration by parents of children with special needs.

All parents should be sensitive to these concerns as we build communities of support for one another.

## Acceptance

Probably one of the most important aspects of parenting a child with special needs is having the child understand that he or she is genuinely valued and accepted by the family. This isn't easy in a society where people constantly compare themselves with one another, against a backdrop of unrealistic ideals such as the perfect-bodied models we see on TV, in movies and in magazines.

When children are old enough to become aware of the differences between themselves and others, questions about whether or not they're "OK" inevitably will be asked. Obvious physical differences probably will arise as an issue at a younger age, but other kinds of differences can also affect a child's sense of self-worth. For example, if all classmates are learning to read and a child just can't seem to get it, feelings of inadequacy can start to influence behavior.

Along these same lines, it takes extra effort on a parent's part to ensure that a child with special needs knows that the attention being given is offered out of love, not because it is required. This subtle difference can only come from the heart, and it can drastically influence a child's ability to value and accept his or her own worth as a human being.

Sometimes children with special needs demand so much extra physical care from parents that the youngsters see themselves as a burden, rather than as a contributing member of a family. Understandably, parents sometimes feel overwhelmed or resent the tremendous responsibilities they bear. Whether it's frequent trips back and forth to the doctor or having to be there for twenty-four-hour care, physical and mental stress are almost inevitable for parents and other caregivers in a family.

Parents sometimes haven't worked through their own feelings of being "helpless" as they stand by and watch their child suffer or endure a painful medical procedure. Accepting their child's limitations has a strong influence on how the child adjusts to disability.

However, ways can be found to encourage each child to make a contribution to the well-being of the family and to feel worthy of love. Situations can provide an opportunity for parents to learn, as well as to be creative in working with their child. For example, children who could not use their arms have learned to paint with their toes. Computers and other technology make many things possible today that were unthinkable even ten years ago.

Each of our self-images comes, to a great extent, from the feedback we get from those around us. A pat on the back for trying to accomplish things can provide motivation for challenging situations. Framing realistic expectations without unnecessarily limiting them is a continuous balancing act. Ignoring or minimizing attention to failures can help. Parental attitude will inevitably influence the attitude children take in living with special needs and their willingness to strive to be the best that they can be.

For parents of children with special needs, balancing positive expectations with realistic limitations is never easy. There is a tendency across society for people to underestimate rather than overestimate others' abilities. When physical limitations are present, the tendency defies reality even more. Presumptions about what others are able to understand about what is going on around them are frequently proven wrong. Even if a person can't respond directly, we all need to be more conscious of the remarks we make and the attitudes we project.

I knew a young man who received numerous injuries when attacked by a group of youngsters who stole his bike. He was unconscious for over six months. Family and friends continued to visit him, to read to him, to talk to him throughout this time. When he became conscious, he had to relearn everything, but he went on to become a productive member of society. I have no doubt that all the positive unconscious input assisted in saving his life.

The tendency for adults to talk about children as if they weren't present — in front of them — needs to be countered whenever possible by parents.

## Dealing with Environmental Limitations

Only in recent years have we become conscious of the need to make public places more accessible to people with physical disabilities. Still more consciousness among the general public regarding the importance of respecting  parking places for the handicapped and developing easy access is needed.

More unisex bathrooms and locker facilities are needed  for people with disabilities, whose caregivers are not necessarily of the same gender. Awkward situations are almost unavoidable under current circumstances. For example, a ten-year-old autistic boy may have no consciousness whatsoever about gender differences, but people are still offended or embarrassed if female caregivers bring him into the girl's locker room to change into a swimming suit.

We also tend to be intolerant of differences in behavior. Children who do not conform within the norm are often judged harshly. Parents of children with disabilities must be prepared to act assertively in answering questions or defending their child's right to participate in community activities. Children also need assistance in learning to answer questions about a disability. Strangers often feel awkward and don't choose appropriate things to say, although they usually mean no harm. Being straightforward rather than defensive often works best. Role playing can go a long way in building confidence about how to respond. The impact of hurt feelings caused by insensitive comments from others can also be minimized through regular honest discussion about such behavior and consistent assurance of worth.

## Coping Strategies

**Encouraging responsibility:** Facing limitations can seriously undermine a child's self-confidence. Encouraging a child to take care of himself or herself whenever possible allows the child opportunities to gain some sense of control over their lives. Extra effort may be required to allow a child time to dress or eat, but the long-term rewards can be invaluable. For a child who often is at the mercy of medical personnel who are doing surgery, administering therapy or medicine, or analyzing problems, offering a child the chance to make choices and to meet his or her own basic needs is very significant. It also presents a chance for parents to reinforce a child's accomplishment.

Frustration and failure occur more frequently among children with disabilities, adding importance to a healthy perspective in managing challenges. Just as it's common for a two-year-old to throw a temper tantrum when he or she is unable to accomplish something, intense frustration might be common if a child has a physical disability. Modeling and guidance by parents can provide a healthy structure for dealing with disappointment or failure. Pounding a pillow, yelling outside or in his or her room or stomping feet can be acceptable alternatives for a child to express anger.

Parents of children with special needs shouldn't hesitate to set clear limits. A disability isn't an excuse for behavior that is destructive, disrespectful or harmful to others. If such negative behavior is tolerated, the child's self-concept will suffer, as well as the family and community.

When a child with a disability has brothers and sisters, resentment is less likely if rules for behavior are as similar as possible for the entire family. Carrying a fair share of family responsibilities when it comes to chores also builds character and minimizes the resentment siblings might feel about all the "attention" given a child with a disability. As with children of different ages, tasks need to match abilities. However, try not to underestimate what's possible. Giving a child specific responsibilities sends the message that you feel the child is a capable person, which builds confidence. No one can learn to take care of himself or herself unless given the opportunity to do so. Necessary tasks can often be made appropriate by incorporating a little creativity. With the special equipment available today, many disabled individuals function entirely on their own.

Doing "good deeds" or making things for others presents opportunities for any child to get positive feedback. The smile on your face when you're given such a "work of art" says a lot more than we often express with words.

**Peer Relationships**

Children with disabilities interact regularly with adults, particularly medical personnel, but their exposure to children their own age is sometimes limited. Most disabled children, however, need to interact with their peers as much as other children. Unfortunately, a child in a wheelchair cannot get around alone in a community as easily as others. Parents must put forth extra effort so their disabled child has a chance to interact successfully with his or her peers.

Rewards for the extra effort can be great for parents and kids alike. Kids develop social skills and are stimulated, challenged and entertained through contact with their peers. Interaction gives them new ways of looking at things and new knowledge to share. For parents, it offers some relief from being the primary source of stimulation for their child. Although children with disabilities sometimes attend special schools, more and more are being mainstreamed and are progressing well in standard public schools. Kids in wheelchairs, those with bald heads from cancer treatments or arms that end at the elbow are becoming more familiar as classmates in many schools. This, in turn, enables children to become more understanding and accepting of differences among community members.

As with any teen, the question of peer relationships and independence becomes more intense with age. Encouraging youth to make their own decisions about friends, clothes and activities gains significance. Involving teens in making medical and educational choices can help them feel a greater sense of power and control. Exploring how their disability affects their lives and learning to speak up for themselves in terms of deciding when, how or if they want assistance from others is also important. This gradual process not only provides experience in handling responsibility and taking risks, but also in accepting the consequences of actions.

## Taking Care of Yourself

Parents must remember to safeguard their own physical and mental health, as well as that of their children. Being organized can help. Establishing regular routines assists a child in knowing what to expect. For example, less resistance might be shown for trips to the doctor if a child knows that afterward you'll do something fun or special together — even something as simple as a trip to the ice cream shop. If medical appointments, school meetings or therapy are frequent, a daily planner can help you keep track of what's next.

Don't hesitate to recruit help from others when possible. Every parent needs regular breaks from the responsibilities of child care. Because the demands on parents of children with a disability are sometimes even greater than what's required of other parents, regular evaluation is useful. Exchange child care with other parents, when possible. Services such as Respite care, Children's Special Health Care Services, Supplemental Security Income (S.S.I., a governmental program), Early Intervention Services, Public Health Nurse Services, Vocational Rehabilitation Services, nonprofit organizations who offer independent living services, Medicaid and Medicare are also possible resources for parents of a child with a disability.

Parents who take the time to maintain their own adult relationships can bring a more positive attitude to time spent with children. Talking with friends or your spouse about your feelings on a regular basis or joining a support group for folks facing similar circumstances can be invaluable. It might also increase your knowledge of the disability your child faces and what might be expected in the course of treatment. Reading is another great source of confidence and learning about your child's disability.

Many families at some point could use professional help in dealing with critical issues or working out healthier ways to interact. If insurance doesn't cover this kind of assistance, many cities have nonprofit organizations that charge according to ability to pay or nothing at all.

High stress situations tend to make people forget that having fun needs to be a regular part of everyone's life. Singing, tickling, laughing, hugging, using imagination and playing games can be great tension reducers. Be sure that you carve out a special time to share love with each person in your family regularly.

*~ The Parenting Tightrope ~*

# ~ *Chapter Seventeen* ~

# **Drugs**

Although it's not always recognized as the culprit, substance abuse probably is our single greatest cause of crisis.

In the extreme, death of an abuser not only leads to grief for family and friends but burdens children with growing up minus one or both parents. Children whose parents abuse substances are usually unable to trust and have a fear of commitment. The pending crisis of an abuser becoming unconscious or violent looms over families. Children can react to a lack of nurturing by striking out at others, failing to concentrate in school or being unable to socialize in appropriate ways.

Many crimes of violence and theft can be directly traced to drug traffic, use and addiction. Not only does this cause crisis for the crime victims, but it wastes millions of our tax dollars in efforts to catch, prosecute and house these criminals. To many, the true crime is the economic burden of sustaining them is prison rather than having them be productive members of society.

The abuse of substances is not confined to large cities or particular cultural groupings. It permeates our entire society. Children of abusers can be found in almost every school in this country.

So, how can parents gain some perspective on this situation? What are our children exposed to about drugs?

## The Big Picture

Drugs, used properly, produce amazing, positive results. Over-the-counter drugs relieve many simple aches and pains. Childhood diseases that killed thousands now are preventable, manageable or curable because of pharmacological science.

At the same time, we have developed a crutchlike dependence on even legitimate drugs — a sense that a pill or a capsule can solve most any hurt. We are bombarded with messages about drugs, both "good" and "bad."

- Instant relief!
- Lose weight the easy way!
- Want to look sexy and sophisticated?
  Smoke cigarettes!
- Want to be attractive and have fun? Drink alcohol.

We don't see TV commercials for illicit substances. But is it such a great leap for children to get messages such as:

- Don't seem to be accepted by peers? Try drugs.
- Lack confidence before a test or contest? Drugs
  can offer support.
- Are you feeling unhappy? Drugs can help you
  ignore things.

These are not the kinds of messages parents would choose for their children to be getting, but this is often what is perceived. Messages concerning alcohol are particularly confusing. Alcohol is used symbolically in many religious ceremonies and has long been an acceptable rite of passage when a young person reaches legal age. Boundaries defining alcohol use and alcohol abuse are far from clear.

## Denial

Part of what makes addictive substances so difficult to deal with is that denial of the problem is so strong. Some communities used to resist even addressing drug abuse on grounds that no one in their schools had such a problem. Fewer institutions are putting their heads in the sand these days, however. Denial tends to be more individualized.

Adults with problems often claim they could quit substance abuse any time or that their use is not affecting their lives. Similarly, youth deny and don't recognize the heightened damage that alcohol can do to bodies that are still developing. The common perception among youth that nothing bad is ever going to happen to them is particularly popular when it comes to substance abuse. Pressure from peers to "have fun" drinking or to be "part of the crowd" by trying an assortment of drugs can be hard to resist.

A video shown at my doctor's office estimated that there are more than seventy-five thousand American youth under age eighteen are alcoholics. Newspaper articles regularly report deaths from drug overdoses or statistics indicating that smoking and alcohol are atop our nation's list of killers. These messages don't reach our children nearly as often as the bogus glamor of tobacco and alcohol portrayed on TV and in print advertising.

## Possible Parent Actions

Preventing our children from ever engaging in substance abuse is by far the healthiest path, obviously. But how in the world can we effectively steer them toward the healthy choice?

Balancing when and how we talk to our children about this subject, as well as what we say, often leaves parents tongue-tied.

But there is hope. A report by the Search Institute indicates that even though it is often assumed that teens tend to get their strongest influence from their peers, in reality parents still have the most influence on teen behavior.

As a good first step, parents can examine their own behavior and think about the messages they send to youth about alcohol or other drug use. Modeling healthy choices can go a long way in helping youngsters develop their own sense of values.

Keeping two-way communication open between parents and youth not only encourages more positive self-esteem, but offers the opportunity to evaluate and share opinions and experiences about the issue of drugs. Discussing something you see on TV or in the newspaper can serve as a catalyst. Make sure that you take the time to make clear what you feel is a healthy approach to the use of alcohol and other drugs, and offer youngsters the opportunity to question the basis for your opinions while expressing their own.

Regardless of how much you would like to control your youngsters' behavior, choices inevitably will arise that each youngster must face alone. Constructive guidance is more likely to have a lasting effect than demands or orders.

Making sure that your child has adequate information is also extremely important. Telling youth to "just say no" is not adequate.

Alcohol and tobacco are the most easily accessible drugs, because their use by adults is legal. Surveys in several communities have indicated that high school youths were easily able to buy liquor themselves from many stores. Vending machines make obtaining cigarettes even easier.

Youth need to understand that alcohol is a depressant. It slows the central nervous system. In simple terms, if you drink too much, too fast, you will kill yourself. The "friends" who took one sixteen-year-old out on her birthday and encouraged her to drink most of a fifth of whiskey didn't know she was going to die, but she did. Her heart just stopped.

As much as we might wish it, demanding our kids *not* drink isn't likely to be effective. Alcohol use is too thoroughly ingrained in our society. Kids associate alcohol with sophistication, with "growing up" — and think they *can't* become addicted. That's long-term. Short-term, youthful abusers engage in chug-a-lugging contests and drinking to get drunk. When they get behind the wheel of a car, they have a short-term *fatal* problem.

Pragmatically, youth must be educated to understand that reasonable guidelines for preventing alcoholism in adults with no health problems or family history demand:

- No more than one drink per hour.
- No more than three drinks in any one day.

It also needs to be made clear that physical health, body size, when food was eaten, family history and genetic make-up are also important in deciding how much alcohol can be consumed relatively safely. With this knowledge, at least youngsters will be more conscious of the dangers of alcoholism and might temper the damage they choose to do to themselves.

Youth-to-youth groups are being developed in many schools to sponsor fun activities that specifically don't involve alcohol or other drugs. Supporting these types of healthy opportunities is strategically important for parents.

Tobacco use by teens is an even more insidious problem in the sense that the consequences are almost all long-term.

Many people don't realize it, but nicotine is one of the most addictive substances on the face of the Earth. Once started, breaking the smoking habit is a clinical nightmare for many people. Worst of all, smoking not only can kill the smoker but can cause serious health problems for his or her companions.

## Illegal Drug Use

The messages surrounding the use of various illegal drugs are not as confusing to most youngsters as the use of legal drugs. The media make clear that drugs such as crack and cocaine can kill. Less clear are some other facts, such as the higher amount of THC (the chief mind-altering ingredient, delta-9-tetrahydrocannabinol) in marijuana today than when the drug became widely used in the '60s.

One of the most important facts for youngsters to understand is that they never can be sure what they're getting if they buy illegal drugs on the street. Everything from rat poison to various hallucinatory drugs has been passed off as something else. "Designer" drugs, slightly different in molecular structure from abused prescription drugs, finally have been made illegal. But an amazing variety of substances are still being peddled to youth susceptible to appeals for something that will make them *high*.

Some signs that might signal a youngster who is using drugs include:

- Drastic mood swings.
- Changes in performance in school or in sports.
- Association with known abusers in the community.

Denial is characteristic of substance abuse. False accusations, however, can set up significant roadblocks, so parents need to approach this issue with a sincere intent to learn — to find out if there is a problem and, if so, what can be done turn the situation in healthier directions.

*~ The Parenting Tightrope ~*

# ~ *Chapter Eighteen* ~

# **Sexuality**

A woman walks into a public swimming pool. She puts her bag down on a beach chair and begins to take off her clothes and change into her swimsuit. When lifeguards notice what's going on, they immediately make her cover her body, then direct her to the women's locker room.

This woman was from Sweden, and she was only practicing what Swedes do every day without a second thought. Seeing other people's bodies is not a big deal — after all, everyone has one. Customs vary greatly around the world. In some countries, public nudity is a fact of life. In others, women are required to cover even their faces in public. As our society grows continuously more diversified, almost every cultural attitude toward sex is represented in our communities. At the same time, our entertainment and advertising media exploit sex at every turn. Against this backdrop, a parent must make individual choices about how, when and what to teach children about sexuality.

Is it OK for young children of different sexes to swim together nude in the backyard pool? When I was growing up, it seemed a big deal to a group of giggly girls for some seven-year-old boys to display their penises from the bushes on the playground. To me, it merely seemed kind of dumb. I had a one-year-old brother at the time. Seeing a penis was an everyday occurrence in our house, as I watched diapers being changed. But how do parents decide what's appropriate? How much should we tell youth as they approach sexual maturity? How do we let our youngsters be comfortable and proud of their bodies, yet teach them not to take advantage of others and to protect themselves from being taken unfair advantage of?

Is sexuality an appropriate topic for a parenting book? Of course. Parents' attitudes will have implications for years to come on a society that already has great difficulty dealing with this topic. Contradictory messages and hurt are too commonly connected to gender. Educating our children consciously, after giving careful consideration to our own values, is an important part of the parenting task.

I first began to wonder consciously about society's values regarding our bodies when I was around four years old. Kids my age made fun of others when they saw their underwear. ("I see London, I see France ...") I didn't understand why it was a problem. Underwear was one layer of clothing over a body just like a bathing suit, and no one made fun of people at swimming pools. But I didn't want to get teased, so I began to be careful about keeping my dress pulled down to my knees and only turning upside down when no boys were around. Already the subject was getting complicated.

Today, our abominable rate of teen pregnancy is proof enough that we are not adequately dealing with the question of sexuality. The well-documented risks to babies of teen mothers are tremendously higher than for babies born to older parents. Teens tend to have difficulty dealing with their own emotional development, let alone meeting the numerous demands of new motherhood. Add to this that there is frequently no help or support from the baby's father and the situation becomes even more difficult.

All parents already know something about sexuality or they wouldn't be parents. However, knowing something about sex and talking about it with your youngsters are two different issues. Research shows that open communication tends to deter youth from becoming parents prematurely.

## Parental Strategies

Children are naturally curious about their own bodies and those of others. Sharing affection is also a major part of the nurturing process. But what are reasonable boundaries? Knowing what information to share, and when, is one of the most difficult tasks of parenthood. There is no "right" answer for all situations and all families.

However, parents need to remember when children ask questions to keep their initial answers simple. Many people have probably heard the story about the child who asked "Mommy, where did I come from?" Without further ado, the parent proceeded to give a detailed biological explanation about the fertilization and birth process. Later, the parent discovered the child was requesting the name of the city where he was born. Children will ask further questions, if need be.

Other things to keep in mind when discussing sexuality include:

- Use proper terminology for body parts.
- Give information in a straightforward manner that does not indicate embarrassment or shame.
- Use questions as an opportunity to share with youngsters how to care for, value and respect bodies.

As children come into contact with others, additional challenges sometimes arise. For example, what action is appropriate for parents when your child shares with you that a four-year-old boy has been attempting to imitate with his preschool classmates the positioning and touching that he saw in nude pictures in his teen cousin's room? Similarly, what about when a seven-year-old girl tries to involve her playmates of the same sex in imagining and imitating the movements she saw in love-making scenes from an X-rated movie? It's almost inevitable that every parent will have to deal with such a situation at some point.

Although the specifics will vary, it's important for parents to think about what they want to accomplish.

After considering the physical and mental well-being of all involved, talking to youngsters directly, their parents or other supervisory personnel — such as teachers or daycare providers — might be appropriate action to take.

Children also can be specifically taught how to deal with situations that make them uncomfortable. For example, aside from telling children to let appropriate people know when there are questionable activities going on, role playing what to say if someone makes you feel uncomfortable is good preparation for life. Let children know that anytime someone asks you not to tell anyone about what you're doing or to keep a secret about touching private parts, it's time to get help from someone they trust.

Parents need to use careful self-control in their reaction to anything a child might reveal. An extreme reaction can discourage a child from ever sharing such information again. Children need to know that we are there to offer assistance and protection in a responsible way.

Parents can also help children learn to differentiate between mere physical attraction and sexual relationships. The media tends to fuse the two, often in a negative way. Parents can promote the concept of sexual relationships as a natural part of life, based on respect and caring, rather than as a strictly physical act.

Probably one of the best defenses to the barrage of negative perspectives on sexuality is encouraging children to feel confident about themselves and their right to protect themselves from any uncomfortable feelings or touches, to know that their bodies are to be valued and respected by themselves and by others. A discussion about what this means specifically is necessary as a child enters each developmental stage.

Our communities can assist in educating children about reasonable boundaries for comfortable and uncomfortable touch. It's important for children to understand that sometimes it is necessary for medical personnel or parents to touch their private parts, for cleaning or examination or treatment of a problem. We want to try to prevent panic or exaggeration regarding what might happen during routine care. But abuse by a caregiver — whether a baby sitter, a relative or a neighbor — is far more common than recognized and we must guard against it.

In the local schools where I live, a play about "touch" is presented for elementary school. Classroom programs with puppets are presented as a follow-up to clarify for children what is acceptable in our society according to our laws.

As children grow, maintaining open communication around sexual issues is critical. The surgeon general under the Reagan administration sent out letters to all parents urging them to talk to their children about AIDS. The cost of sexually transmitted diseases to this society, in terms of dollars spent on treatment and the hurt to friends and family members, is immense and incredible.

Teens, particularly, have a tendency to believe "nothing bad could ever happen to me." Experimenting with relationships and becoming comfortable with their adult bodies is part of the growing process. Unfortunately, date/acquaintance rape is far too common. The number of young AIDS victims is growing quickly. According to the U.S. Center for Disease Control, forty percent of people in the United States with AIDS are heterosexuals. Parents need to become informed about the facts and myths surrounding this disease and educate their children about protective measures.

Parents can also try to encourage the media to produce more healthy entertainment for our children. Unfortunately, sex, detached from the concept of caring relationships, sells. The enormous amounts of money tied up in advertising will make it difficult, but not impossible, to influence the media. Humor and tenderness also sell. Parents in a coalition could send a strong message to advertisers about what they want their children to see. Maybe it's time to start changing the self-esteem of this nation as a whole and encouraging it to present itself in a more positive light.

Parents can provide the base for this change by:

- Making sure they model healthy attitudes about relationships and gender differences.
- Discussing realistic standards for behavior, teaching decision-making skills, and doing roleplays that help children protect their bodies.
- Providing correct information, as needed, on sexual issues.
- Promoting respect for the rights of others.

Families can provide the first environment in which youngsters learn about the emotional side of truly loving relationships.

## ~ *Part Three* ~

# Putting It All Together

I often think of parents as holding umbrellas over our children, attempting to shelter them from harm, yet allowing them the freedom to experiment within healthy boundaries. Those boundaries today, however, tend to have a very wide range. Parents can't realistically isolate their children from community influence — nor would that be appropriate. Nevertheless, understanding the African proverb "it takes a whole village to raise a child" brings up the question of what kind of atmosphere the *village* has. How can parents enlist the help of others in the challenging task of ensuring that the environment surrounding our children is safe and healthy.

This section will look at actions parent can take to strengthen full community involvement and commitment to the well-being of children in our neighborhoods. It will also discuss how parents can network and utilize the many resources that communities offer to support child-rearing efforts.

*~ The Parenting Tightrope ~*

## ~ *Chapter Nineteen* ~

# A Community Effort

**P**arents play a critical role in setting the tone for what's acceptable in our neighborhoods. It's important to remember that there is a tendency for others to treat our children the way we do. If child-care providers, teachers, neighbors or other youth see us disrespecting our children, there's a tendency to feel it's OK for them to treat youth in the same disrespectful ways.

Too often in our neighborhoods, youngsters spend their time taunting one another and bragging about how hurtful they can be. This is true in all kinds of neighborhoods, regardless of socio-economic levels. Something is wrong with a society in which being cruel is so common as a way of relating to one another.

Most topics I have addressed in this book point to the fact that if we want our world to move toward being a healthier place, parents need to become the peacemakers:

- Peacemakers in terms of what we model for our children in learning to interact and get along with others in the community.
- Peacemakers in terms of training our children specifically to be more humane in their treatment of others.

- Peacemakers in terms of truly understanding the connection between individual acts and the health of the community as a whole.

However, if we want a more peaceful, healthier atmosphere to become a reality, it will be necessary to encourage coordinated efforts within our communities.

People sometimes say that they want things to change, but they don't know what to do. I firmly believe that we do know what to do. Much research on successful efforts to move communities in healthier directions has been compiled.

For example, Dr. James Comer of the Yale University Child Studies Center has documented the significant difference the "Comer process" can make. This process requires including input from all school "stakeholders" in decision making. Parents, teachers, administrators, human service agencies and businesses all have been involved in the development of plans enabling the atmosphere in schools to become nurturing and conducive to learning. Even children from the lowest economic neighborhoods have shown remarkable improvement in both attitude and test performance as a result of this cooperative orientation. Although not officially documented as attributable to the Comer process, crime in the neighborhoods using this program has also declined.

Overall, many schools in our educational system don't address critical areas that affect entire communities. Besides academics, each community school curriculum should include training in communication and problem-solving skills and set clear standards of acceptable behavior. Children who feel unsafe cannot concentrate on learning. Peer mediators have been effectively used in numerous schools to assist in resolving student disputes. Because many students face high-stress situations at some point, student assistance groups can offer support and serve as a liaison between the school and community human services when additional help is needed.

Partnerships with community businesses and law enforcement agencies can also contribute to an overall atmosphere of cooperation and community involvement. Mentoring programs familiarize students with community occupations and promote students' understanding of the contributions they will be able to make as adults. Individual attention also helps develop a child's self-esteem.

Parent involvement in schools is critical. Offering educational classes to parents on such topics as child development and effective discipline can prove supportive to parents and strengthen the bond between parents and schools. Support groups for parents can also be offered in the community through religious organizations, human service agencies or block clubs. Opportunities for parents to donate their expertise and time to classroom activities can also be invaluable. For instance, parents at my children's school help print student-written books on a computer, share their travel stories, sing and assist with reading activities.

Common Ground's Prevention Unit has developed materials that can assist in the process of re-orienting schools in healthy directions. Our Peer Relationships program includes experiential exercises to encourage healthy interaction, both at home and school. Watch Me Grow and Project Self are more comprehensive student assistance programs for 3rd to 12th graders.

An office of the federal government has published a book titled *The Future by Design*. It includes specific step-by-step instructions for organizing communities to decide consciously the direction in which they want to move and how to get there. Someone must take the initiative. It will then take a commitment from government, institutions, businesses and families to promote significant change. It can be done.

Together, we can shape the future to a great extent. We each need to be actively conscious of exactly what we're creating and remember that:

- Mistakes are best dealt with as opportunities for learning with children and in the community.
- Flexibility within reasonable boundaries is basic to the tough job of parenting and to move forward cooperatively as a society.

*~ Chapter Twenty ~*

# Parental Support and Community Resources

I t's Friday afternoon at the end of a hectic week. Deadlines have kept pressure on you at work. Driving home, you know the kids are going to be hungry and tired. You face the prospect of fixing dinner, doing dishes, bathing youngsters and starting to work through the mountain of laundry in the basement. And you are supposed to have a positive attitude — to be loving, patient and creative with whining kids.

Such a minicrisis can leave a parent feeling there's no way out. However, a vision of light at the end of this tunnel is possible if you take just a few minutes to think:

- Could dinner be made more simple by using leftovers or something frozen?
- Is going out to dinner or getting a carry-out possible? (The kids might be thrilled.)

- Are there neighbor kids who might play with your children so at least you can fix dinner in peace?
- Is there a friend or relative you could visit or call to let you get the week's frustration off your chest before doing anything else?
- Could you give the kids a granola bar or have a family hug when you first hit the door so that waiting for dinner won't seem so bad?

Parents all need a backup occasionally. A major part of the parental balancing act is taking care of your needs, as well as those of the kids. Giving yourself a bit of a break can help relieve pressure from the rigors of parenting.

Aside from the needs and responsibilities that every adult has — such as feeling what they do is worthwhile and having adequate food, clothing and shelter — let's consider for a minute the needs that are sometimes more difficult for parents to meet:

- Time for a healthy, adult romantic relationship.
- Time to have adult friendships.
- Private time to relax or take care of your physical and mental well-being.

When I talk with parents, not enough time is probably the most common complaint I hear, particularly in families in which both parents work or in single-parent families.

But organizing is very important for all parents — not just in terms of time, but in terms of having the social support we need to function effectively as parents.

As we get into the specifics, it is important to keep in mind that developing a successful support system requires "give" and "take," just as any healthy relationship does. However, taking initiative and making the effort to put community connections in place is very worthwhile in the long run.

## Getting Started

Some people are fortunate enough to have relatives or a well-established group of friends when they become pregnant. Information from those friends about their experiences as parents can be invaluable. It's also nice to involve them in sharing the changes experienced as the baby grows. This encourages a sense of closeness to the baby before he or she even arrives. However, new parents in our very mobile society often don't have these traditional support systems. So where's a good place to start building alternatives?

Even before the birth of a child, relationships with other families can be built through child-birth preparation or Lamaze classes. Local offerings are usually listed in the yellow pages under "Childbirth." Human service agencies and hospitals also frequently have classes. Fees vary, but health departments in particular try to make programs available for free or at minimal cost to anyone interested.

Not only does this training make the birthing process easier, but the knowledge provided can give parents more confidence in handling the first few critical weeks of taking care of their baby. Teachers are often accessible for questions or will give you telephone numbers of someone who can answer baby questions in your community. New-parent support groups can be helpful, as well. Classes are also frequently available through human service agencies for adoptive parents.

After parents have gotten somewhat accustomed to their new family member and have established basic routines, beginning some structured fun activities can offer a break for both baby and parent. Human service agencies or recreation departments might offer such things as parent-infant water classes or movement exploration. Taking your baby for a stroller walk outside or at the mall can get you some exercise and offer your child the stimulation of new surroundings. Libraries are another pleasant place in which a wealth of information on newborns can be found. Each of these activities also offers the opportunity for you to meet other parents in your community with whom you might begin to share ideas, activities — or even babysitting — after you get to know them.

Your toddler tugs on your pants as you wash the dishes and says, "I want you to play with me!" You might wish to stop what you're doing and play whenever your child asks, but it's frequently not practical or even possible. However, parents need to keep in mind that the first few years are critical in the development of how children feel about themselves. If children are constantly put off because of other demands or aren't getting enough quality interaction with others, it can cause problems. Luckily, some of that quality interaction can come from others.

Parents need to balance time with children and time without them. If parents take breaks from their children, it's much easier to have a nurturing relationship during the many hours you're together. This is true whether parents are formally employed or do not work outside the home. It's best if time with children includes not only the necessities such as baths, dressing and feeding, but also special sharing time for reading, singing or playing. (Don't forget that fun can also be incorporated into the necessary activities.) It's also important to see that the time away includes relaxation and tasks that are more easily done without kids.

Some communities are developing more services to assist parents. For example, there are warm, caring places in my area at which you can drop infants or children off for care at an hourly rate. These are listed in the Yellow Pages. Some recreational facilities offer child care while parents take classes or exercise. Licensed daycare homes will sometimes be willing to take children for a regularly scheduled "parent break," as well as providing regular daycare for employed parents. Their rates are often reasonable. Some state departments of social services will mail a list of homes for you to consider.

Until children approach the teen years, all parents must find someone to care for their youngsters when they can't. We have a long way to go in terms of having affordable, healthy, convenient child care readily available for all parents. However, some other options to consider include:

- Asking local schools for a list of neighborhood teens interested in part-time babysitting.
- Putting a help-wanted ad in the local paper, religious bulletin or on the grocery store bulletin board.
- Encouraging larger employers or groups of smaller employers to consider setting up daycare centers near or at your work site.
- Doing telephone networking with any parents you know to find out who does their child care. Ask for referrals.
- Joining or starting a babysitting co-op in your neighborhood that uses time tokens instead of money for care exchange.

Before you leave your child in anyone else's care, be sure to do a personal interview, check out their references and become familiar with the facility where care will be given.

Regardless of whether it's a necessity or not, by the time a child is walking around and beginning to talk, it's a good idea for parents to be consciously planning time for interaction between their youngster and others close to their age. It's easier to involve our kids in activities with other children than to have the demand for attention or stimulation centered primarily on us. It's also useful for them to begin to learn positive social skills at an early age.

## The Elementary Years

By the time children begin school, many new options for care and activities become available. Some schools have before care and after care, tutoring, Scouts or other structured activities on campus. Often classmates live nearby and parents welcome exchanging kids during the afternoons. Libraries sometimes sponsor afternoon programs or have computer games that can be fun, challenging and educational. Recreation departments or Boys and Girls Clubs usually offer a variety of classes, as well as space for exerting energy in constructive ways. Religious organizations may also offer a variety of activities.

Children at this level often have become very adept at entertaining themselves with games, arts and crafts projects or sports. Although TV is often the easiest, most readily available entertainment, resisting the urge to have it on for long hours promotes more creative and intellectually stimulating activities.

Achieving balance among activities, homework, chores and some time for just relaxing is another challenge for parents. Children are often drawn to participate in so many different things that even transportation can put real stress on parents. Overprogrammed lives also leave limited time for family interaction or sharing the basic skills, such as cooking and cleaning, that every child needs to learn. Homework done when kids are already exhausted is more easily frustrating and tends to take longer.

Making a list of the activities in which children want to participate on one side of a page and their family responsibilities on the other side can be the first step in planning what's reasonable. Elementary school children are old enough to be actively involved in making choices. Letting them consider what's most important to them and helping them understand the contribution that is also needed by their family often makes implementing a plan less difficult. Parental guidance within appropriate boundaries promotes learning much more than authoritarian demands.

Schools and human service agencies often offer parenting classes or have counselors available to support your efforts as a parent. Sometimes getting another person's perspective on a family situation can be both enlightening and productive.

## Middle and High School Years

"He comes in from basketball practice, grabs a quick bite to eat and goes to his room. I don't see him again until I go in to say good night."

"She's on the phone nonstop unless she's told to get off. I get two-word answers to questions I ask to show interest in what she's doing."

"He doesn't come home when he says he will, but I don't want to feel that I'm running a jail. He's determined to do whatever he wants to do, without taking anyone else into consideration."

These types of comments from parents of teenagers are all too common. Where can parents turn for support? Again, referrals available from schools and human services organizations can be invaluable. It's also useful to get to know the parents of your teenager's friends. Getting together to talk about what's reasonable in terms of curfew, setting up some specific procedures for spending the night at others' houses or guidelines for parties are just a few of the topics it's useful to discuss.

If every parent could be in a support group that met at least once a week, there'd probably be many fewer problems in our communities. Especially for teenagers, there seems to be a lack of community guidelines for behavior. Respect for others does not seem to be one of the dominant characteristics of our culture. But neither parents, schools, religious organizations nor law enforcement agencies can take sole responsibility for guiding youth. Coordinated efforts are most effective.

Teenagers need to exert their independence, have time to themselves and time to connect with their peers. It's ideal to have parents recognize these factors and not be threatened by them. Yet, parents still must strive to make their presence known enough so that a teen's freedom exists within healthy boundaries. Keeping communication open during these years is challenging, but probably the most useful factor in promoting health.

## Conclusion

As children grow, parents need to stay aware of the resources available to support them in the challenging task of balancing the many issues that inevitably arise. Helping your children see themselves in a healthy, positive light is one of the greatest gifts there is. To each of you, the best in loving and learning together in your families and in helping create a healthier world.

# ~ *Bibliography* ~

The following references may be available through local libraries, book stores or health departments. They are listed according to many of the topics in The Parenting Tightrope.

## Child Development

The Academy of Pediatrics; Division of Publications. *Caring For Your Adolescent, Ages 12-21.* Elkgrove, Ill.

Baron, Bruce. 1983. *What Did You Learn in School Today?: A Comprehensive Guide to Getting the Best Possible Education for Your Children.* New York, N.Y.: Warner Books.

Berla, Nancy. 1989. *The Middle School Years: A Parent's Handbook.* Columbia, Md.: National Committee for Citizens in Education.

Brazelton, T. Berry, Ph.D. 1992. *Touch Points: Your Child's Emotional and Behavioral Development.* Redding, MA: Addison-Wesley.

Brazelton, T. Berry, Ph.D. 1987. *Infant Development* (videorecording). Hollywood, Calif.: Paramount Home Video; Skillman, NJ:Johnson & Johnson.

Culbreth, Judsen, Ed. *Working Mother* (magazine). New York: Lang Communications, L.P.

Dunn and Hargitt, Inc. 1982. *Growing Parent and Growing Child* (monthly newsletter). Lafayette, In.: Dunn & Hargitt, Inc. Lafayette, Ind.

Lansdown, Richard. 1991. *Your Child's Development From Birth to Adolescence: A Complete Guide For Partents.* New York: Knopf: Distributed by Random House.

Ramey, Anna. 1989. *Parenting Preschoolers!* (videorecording). Austin, Tex.: Family Experiences Productions.

Reddicliffe, Steven, ed. Parenting (magazine). USA: Time Inc. Ventures.

Roeper, Annemarie. 1990. *Educating Children For Life: The Modern Learning Community.* Monroe, N.Y.: Trillium Press.

## Conflict and Decision Making

Berry, Joy Wilt. 1987. *Every Kid's Guide to Decision Making and Problem Solving.* Chicago: Childrens Press.

Berry, Joy Wilt. 1982, ©1979. *Making Up Your Own Mind: A Children's Book About Decision Making and Problem Solving.* Chicago: Children's Press.

Crary, Elizabeth. 1983. *A Children's Problem-Solving Series.* Seattle, Wash.: Parenting Press, Inc.

Crary, Elizabeth, 1984. *Kids can Cooperate: A Practical Guide to Teaching Problem Solving.* Seattle, Wash: Parenting Press.

Gifaldi, David. 1993. *Toby Scudder, Ultimate Warrior.* New York: Clarion Books.

Ginott, Haim G. 1965. *Between Parent and Child; New Solutions to Old Problems.* New York: Macmillan.

Hawley, Richard A. 1988. *The Big Issues in the Adolescent Journey.* New York: Walker Publications.

Hechinger, Fred M. 1992. *Fateful Choices, Healthy Youth for the 21st Century.* New York: Carnegie Corporation.

McLenahan Wesson, Carolyn. 1988. *Teen Troubles: How to Keep Them from Becoming Tragedies.* Marble Falls, Texas.: Walker Publications.

Paul, Dr. Jordon, Dr. Margaret Paul, and Bonnie B. Hesse. 1987. *If You Really Loved Me ... From Conflict to Closeness for Everyone Who is a Parent and Everyone Who Has Been a Child.* Minneapolis, Minn.: CompCare Publishers.

Tjosvold, Dean, Mary, and Jenny. 1991. *Love and Anger: Managing Family Conflict.* Coon Rapids, Mich.: Team Media.

## Cultural Differences

Bode, Janet. 1989. *Different Worlds: Interracial and Cross-Cultural Dating.* New York: F. Watts.

Deutsch, Martin. 1968. *Social Class, Race, and Psychological Development.* New York: Holt, Rinehart, and Winston.

Goodman-Malamuthm, Leslie. 1992.*Between Two Worlds: Choices for Grown Children of Jewish-Christian Parents* New York: Pocket Books.

Huesmann, L. Rowell. 1986. *Television and the Aggressive     Child: A Cross-national Comparison.* Hillsdale, N.J.: L. Erlbaum Associates.

Langer, Susanne Katheran Knauth. (1968)-1982. *Mind: an Essay on Human Feeling.* Baltimore: Johns Hopkins Press.

Riesman, David. 1950. *The Lonely Crowd: The Study of the Changing American Character.* New Haven: Yale University Press.

Rosenberg, Roy A. 1988. *Happily Intermarried Authoriative Advice for a Joyous Jewish-Christian Marriage.* New York: Macmillan.

## Effective Discipline

Cline, Foster, M.D., and Jim Fay. 1990. *Parenting with Love and Logic: Teaching Children Responsibility.* Colorado Springs, Co.: Navpress.

Dreyer, Sharon Spredemann. 1985. *The Bookfinder: A Guide to Children'sLiterature About the Needs and Problems of Youth Aged 2-15.* Circle Pines, Minn.: American Guidance Service.

Ginott, Haim G. 1971, 1969. *Between Parent and Child.* New York: Avon.

Gootman, Marilyn E. *How to Teach Your Children Discipline.* Chicago, Ill.

Gordon, Thomas. 1970. *P.E.T.: Parent Effectiveness Training: The Tested New Way to Raise Responsible Children.* New York: McKay.

Gordy Levine, Katherine. 1991. *When Good Kids Do Bad Things.* New York: W.W. Norton.

MacDonald, Betty Bard. 1947. *Mrs. Piggle Wiggle Series.* Phildelphia: J. B. Lippincott.

Wilt, Joy. 1979. Weekly Reader Books: The Ready, Set, Grow Series. Waco, Texas: Educational Products Division, Word Incorporated.

Windell, James. 1991. *Discipline: A Sourcebook of Fifty Failsafe Techniques for Parents.* Collier Books.

Windell, James. 1994. *Eight Weeks to a Well-Behaved Child.* New York: MacMillian

## Divorce

Brown, Laurene Krasny. 1986. *Dinosaurs Divorce.* Boston: Atlantic Monthly Press.

Engel, Margorie L., and Diana Gould. 1992. *The Divorce Decisions Workbook.* New York: McGraw Hill.

Engel, Margorie L.. 1994. *The Divorce Help Source Book.* Detroit: Visible Ink Press.

Fassler, David, Michele Lash, and Sally Ives. 1988. *Changing Families: A Guide for Kids and Grownups.* Burlington, Vt.: Waterfront Books.

Galper Cohen, Miriam. *The Joint Custody Handbook.*

Krementz, Jill. 1988. *How It Feels When Parents Divorce.* New York: Knopf: Distributed by Random House.

Krementz, Jill. 1989. *When Mom and Dad Break Up* (videorecording). Hollywood, Calif.: Paramount Home Video.

Newman, George. 1981. *One Hundred and One Ways to be a Long-Distance Super Dad.* Mountain View, Calif: Blossom Valley Press.

Prokop, Michael S. 1986. *Divorce Happens to the Nicest Kids: A Self Help Book For Kids (3-15) and Adults.* Warren, Ohio: Alegra House.

Ricci, Isolina. 1980. *Mom's House, Dad's House.* New York: Macmillan.

## Domestic Violence

Bernstein, Sharon Chesler. 1991. *A Family That Fights.* Morton Grove, Ill.: A. Whitman.

Evans, Patricia. 1992. *The Verbally Abusive Relationship: HowW to Recognize it and How to Respond.* Holbrook, Mass.: Bob Adams.

Gelles, Richard J.. 1985. *Intimate Violence in Families.* Beverly Hills, Calif.: Sage Publications.

Shupe, Anson D.. 1987. *Violent Men, Violent Couples: The Dynamics of Domestic Violence.* Lexington, Mass.: Lexington Books.

## Grief

Adler, C.S. (Carole S.). 1990. *Ghost Brother.* New York: Clarion Books.

Heegaard, Marge Eaton. 1990. *Coping with Death & Grief.* Minneapolis: Lerner Publications.

James, John W.. 1988. *The Grief Recovery Handbook: A Step-by-Step Program For Moving Beyond Loss.* New York: Harper & Row.

LeShan, Eda. 1976. *Learning to Say Good-By.* New York: MacMillan.

Menten, Theodore. 1991. *Gentle Closings: How to Say Goodbye to Someone You Love.* Philadelphia, Pa.:Running Press.

Nieburg, Herbert A.. 1982. *Pet Loss: A Thoughtful Guide for Adults and Children.* New York: Harper & Row.

Staudacher, Carol. 1991. *Men & Grief: A Guide for Men Ssurviving the Death of a Loved One: A Resource for Caregivers and Mental Health Professionals.* Oakland, CA: New Harbinger Publications.

Wiersbe, David. 1992. *Gone But Not Lost: Grieving the Death of a Child.* Grand Rapids, Mich: Baker Book House.

Williamson, Walter. 1987. *Misscarriage: Sharing the Grief, Facing the Pain, Healing the Wounds.* New York: Walker.

Wright, Betty Ren.. 1991. *The Cat Next Door.* New York: Holiday House.

## Self-Esteem

Clemes, Harris, Ph.D., and Reynold Bean, Ed.M. 1985. *How to Raise Children's Self-Esteem.* Los Angeles, Calif.: Enrich.

Corkville Briggs, Dorothy. 1975. *Your Child's Self-Esteem.* Doubleday & Company.

Cutright, Melitta, Ph.D. 1992. *Growing Up Confident: How to Make Your Child's Early Years Learning Years.* Doubleday.

Dale, L.P., and W. Lang. 1993. Working Mother. New York, N.Y.: Lang Communications.

Friedmann, Barb, and Cheri Brooks. 1990. *On Base! The Step-by-Step Self-Esteem Program for Children from Birth to 18.* Westport Publishers.

Hart, Louise. 1990. *The Winning Family.* Lifeskills Press.

Johnson, Julie Tallard. 1991. *Celebrate You!: Building Your Self-Esteem.* Minneapolis: Lerner Publications.

Youngs, Bettie B., Ph.D. 1991. *The Six Vital Ingredients of Self-Esteem and How to Develop Them in Your Child.* Rawson Associates.

## Sexuality

Eagle, Carol K.. 1993. *All That She Can Be: Helping Your Daughter Achieve Her Full Potential and Maintain Her Self-Esteem During the Critical Years of Adolescence.* New York: Simon & Schuster.

Glassman, Bruce. 1991. *Everything You Need to Know About Growing Up Male.* New York: Rosen.

Koch, Joanne. 1992. *Good Parents for Hard Times: Raising Responsible Kids in the Age of Drug Use and Early Sexual Activity.* New York: Simon & Schuster.

Madaras, Lynda. 1987. *The What's Happening to My Body for Girls: A Growing Up Guide For Parents and Daughters.* New York: New Marbit Press.

## Siblings

Bank, Stephen P.. 1982. *The Sibling Bond.* New York: Basic Books.

Berenstain, Stan. 1986. *The Berenstain Bears: No Girls Allowed.* New York: Random House.

Berry, Joy Wilt. ©1987. *Teach Me Aaout Brothers and Sisters.* Chicago: Childrens Press.

Cleaver, Vera. 1981. *The Kissimmee Kid.* New York: Lothrop, Lee & Shepard.

Faber, Adele. 1987. *Siblings Without Rivalry: How to Help Your Children Live Together so You Can Live Too.* New York: Norton.

Hoopes, Lyn Littlefield. 1983. *When I Was Little.* New York: Dutton.

Klagebrun, Francine. 1992. *Mixed Feelings: Love, Hate, Rivalry, and Reconciliation Among Brothers and Sisters.* New York: Bantan Books.

Powledge, Fred. 1986. *You'll Survive!: Late Blooming, Early Blooming, Lonliness, Klutziness, and Other Problems of Adolescence, and How to Live Through Them.* New York: Scribner.

Stein, Sara Bonnett. 1974. *That New Baby.* New York: Walker.

Tripp, Valerie. 1986. *Meet Molly: An American Girl.* Madison, Wis.: Pleasant Co.

Twerski, Abraham J.. 1992. *I Didn't Ask to Be in This Family: Sibling Relationships and How They Shape Adult Behavior and Relationships.* New York: Topper Books.

Watson, Jane Werner. 1977, ©1992. *Sometime's I'm Jealous.* New York: Golden Press.

Wittman, Sally. 1990. *Jessie's Wishes.* New York: Scholastic, Inc.

## Children with Special Needs

Blank, Joseph P.. 1976. *19 Steps Up the Mountain: the Story of the DeBolt Family.* Philadelphia: Lippincott.

Deppe, Phillip R.. 1981. *The High-Risk Child: A Guide for Concerned Parents.* New York: Macmillan.

Dickman, Irving R.. 1985. *One Miracle at a Time: How to Get Help for Your Disabled Child—From the Experience of Other Children.* New York: Simon & Schuster.

Dwight, Laura. 1992. *We Can Do It!* New York: Checkerboard Press.

Feuer, Elizabeth. 1990. *Paper Doll.* New York: Farrat, Straus, Giroux.

Finston, Peggy. 1990. *Parenting Plus: Raising Children With Special Health Needs.* New York: Dutton.

Kurcinka, Mary S.. 1992. *Raising Your Spirited Child: A Guide for Parents Whose Child Is More: Intense, Sensitive, Perceptive, Persistent, Energetic.* New York: HarperCollins.

Mayer, Gina. 1992. *A Very Special Critter.* New York: Golden Book; Racine, Wis.: Western Publishing Co.

Rosenberg, Maxine B.. 1988. *Finding a Way: Living With Exceptional Brothers and Sisters.* New York: Lothrop, Lee & Shepard Books

## Stepfamilies

Stepfamily Association of America. 1989. *Stepfamilies Stepping Ahead: An Eight-Step Program for Successful Family Living.* Lincoln, Neb.: Stepfamily Association of America.

Belovitch, Jeanne. 1987. *Making Remarriage Work.* New York: MacMillan.

Bernstein, Anne C.. 1989. *Yours, Mine, and Ours: How Families Change When Remarried Parents Have a Child Together.* New York: Scribner.

Boyd, Lizi. 1990. *Sam is My Half-Brother.* New York: Viking.

Burns, Cherie. 1985. *Stepmotherhood: How to Survive without Feeling Frustrated, Left Out or Wicked.* Harper Collins.

Gardner, Richard. 1982. *The Boys and Girls Book about Stepfamilies.* Cresskill, N.J.: Creative Therapeutics.

Gorman, Tony. 1983. *Stepfather.* Boulder, Colorado: Gentle Touch Press.

Keshet, Jamie. 1987. *Love and Power in the Stepfamily.* USA: Penguin.

Lofas, Jeannette. 1987. *Everything You Always Wanted to Ask About Stepkids, but Were Afraid to Know* (audio recording). Chicago: + Nightinggale-Conent Audio.

Miller, Mary Jane. 1990. *Me and My Name.* New York: Viking.

Sabo, Marcella M.. 1989. *Whose Kid IisIt Anyway? : And Over 400 Other Questions for Divorcing, Dating and Remarried Families: The Complete Social and Legal Guide for Stepparents, Step-Children, and Stepgrandparents.* Seattle, Wash.: Next Step Pub.

## Substance Abuse

Beattie, Melody. 1989, ©1987. *Codependent No More.* New York: Walker and Co.

Berger, Gilda. 1982. *Addiction: Its Causes, Problems and Treatments.* New York: F. Watts.

Cohen, Susan. 1987. *What You Can Believe About Drugs: An Honest and Unhysterical Guide For Teens.* New York: M. Evans.

Debner, Claudia Bialke. 1985. *Chemical Dependency: Opposing Viewpoints.* St. Paul, Minn.: Greenhaven Press.

DeStefano, Susan. 1991. *Drugs and the Family.* Frederick, Md.: Twenty-First Century Books.

Freeman, Jodi. 1989. *How to Drug-Proof Kids: A Parents Guide to Early Prevention.* Albuquerque, N.M.: The Think Shop.

Gay, Kathlyn. 1992. *Caution! This May Be an Advertisement: A Teen Guide to Advertising.* New York: Franklin Watts.

Glowa, John R. 1986. *Inhalants: The Toxic Fumes.* New York: Chelsea House.

Hyde, Margaret O. 1978. *Kow About Aalcohol.* New York: McGraw-Hill.

Lachance, Laurie L. 1989. *Alcohol, Drugs and Adolescents.* Ann Arbor, Mich.: ERIC.

Peck, M. Scott. 1991. *Addiction, The Sacred Disease* (audio recording). New York, N.Y.: Simon & Schuster Audioworks.

Rogers, Gerald T. 1985. *Lots of Kids Like Us.* (Video recording). Skokie, Ill.: Gerald T. Rogers Productions, Inc.

Rogers, Gerald T. 1986. *Twelve Steps* (video recording). Skokie, Ill.: Gerald T. Rogers Productions, Inc.

Schlesinger, Stephen E. 1988. *Taking Charge: How Families Can Climb Out of the Chaos of Addiction ... And Flourish.* New York: Simon & Schuster.

Seixas, Judith S. 1985. *Children of Alcoholism: A Survivor's Manual.* New York: Crown Publishers.

## Suicide

Gardner, Sandra. 1990. *Teenage Suicide.* Englewood Cliffs, N.J: Julian Messner.

Gordon, Sol. 1988. *When Living Hurts.* Dell Publishing.

Grollman, Earl A. 1988. *Suicide.* Beacon Press.

Hankoff, Leon D. 1978. *The Doctor Talks to You About Understanding and Preventing Suicide A Discussion* (sound recording). Bayside, New York: Soundwords, Inc.

Hyde, Margaret O. 1986. *Suicide: The Hidden Epidemic.* New York: F. Watts.

Kolehmainen, Janet. 1986. *Teen Suicide: A Book for Friends, Family, and Classmates.* Minneapolis: Lerner Publications.

Kunz, Roxanne Brown. 1986. *Feeling Down: The Way Back Up.* Minneapolis, Minn.: Dillon Press.

Madison, Winifred. 1979. *A Portrait of Myself: A Novel.* New York: Random House.

Nunes, Lydia Bojunga. 1991. *Mi Amigo Pintor. My friend the painter.* San Diego: Harcourt Brace Jovanovich.

Wrobleski, Adina. 1990. *Suicide: Why? Eighty-Five Questions and Answers About Suicide.* Minneapolis, Minn.: Afterwards.